Samson and Delilah Plus Twenty

Elizabeth Rodenz

Samson and Delilah Plus Twenty

Copyright © 2023 by Elizabeth Rodenz

All rights reserved

No part of this book may be reproduced or used in any manner without the prior written permission of the copyright owner, except for the use of brief quotations in a book review.

This book is creative non-fiction. It reflects the author's present recollections of experiences over time. Some names have been changed. Some events have been compressed, and some dialogue has been recreated.

Elizabeth Rodenz
Pittsburgh, PA 15232

Printed and published in
the United States of America 2022
10 9 8 7 6 5 4 3 2 1

ISBN: (hardcover)	978-0-9722694-8-3
ISBN: (softcover)	978-0-9722694-7-6
Library of Congress LCCN	2022943586

Samson and Delilah Plus Twenty
A memoir by Elizabeth Rodenz

1. Dogs 2. Memoir 3. Dog Rescue 4. Dog Adoption 5. Dog Training 6. Pets

TABLE OF CONTENTS

Chapter 1	A Leap of Faith	1
Chapter 2	Angel and Lady	9
Chapter 3	Sissy and Snoopy	14
Chapter 4	Jake and Zoey	22
Chapter 5	Happy Ending for Zoey	28
Chapter 6	Annie, Thelma, and Louise	33
Chapter 7	Dear Sweet Bonnie	38
Chapter 8	Puppy Mills and Breeders	45
Chapter 9	A Return and an Arrival	50
Chapter 10	Welcoming Bonnie Back	58
Chapter 11	Stubborn and Cute	60
Chapter 12	The Sweetness of Bella	64
Chapter 13	Indestructible Delilah	69
Chapter 14	Millie and Sallie	74
Chapter 15	For the Love of Millie	81

Chapter 16	Handsome Samson Boy	87
Chapter 17	For the Love of Samson	95
Chapter 18	Delightful Delilah	101
Chapter 19	Fostering Again	108
Chapter 20	Bailey Boy	117
Chapter 21	Bailey Finds a Home	123
Chapter 22	A Puppy—Oh my!	128
Chapter 23	Flossie	135
Chapter 24	Ki-Ann or Something Like…	140
Chapter 25	Saying Goodbye and Hello	147

Prelude

In *Samson and Delilah—My Two Loves*, I shared a synopsis of a poem entitled *The Touch of the Master's Hand*. I believe it's worth repeating.

The poem tells the story of an old violin being auctioned off. The bidding started at $1, then $2, and $3. An old man standing in the back walked to the front of the room, picked up the violin, and began to play it. Beautiful sounds filled the room. When the old man was finished, the auctioneer resumed the bidding.

The bid started at $1,000, then $2,000. Someone asked, "What changed its worth?"

Swiftly came a reply, "The touch of the master's hand."

Parents can inspire their children to soar. Managers can help their employees to succeed. We can touch our partners, spouses, and friends in a special way. You can do all that and more for your dog with your words, voice, and touch.

I wrote this book so people could experience the joys of fostering rescue dogs and volunteering with a rescue group through a story of love and compassion for our best friend.

I wrote this book hoping that people would be inspired to raise their voices in protest of what is happening to dogs every day.

I wrote this book hoping someone who reads this story would be in a position to do something about the breeding laws in their state and enact more laws to protect animals.

The journey with Samson and Delilah and their foster friends takes roads not traveled and combines stories of rescuing, fostering, training, and advocating, plus a philosophy about our regard for dogs.

Samson and Delilah and their friends are not hero dogs, but they are heroes to the people who rescue them, giving them joy and unconditional love every day.

I hope this book will inspire people to adopt dogs and not buy puppies and dogs, volunteer with rescue organizations, and emerge as an advocate for changing dog laws, especially those regarding breeding, puppy mills, and dogs in laboratories.

I hope you enjoy the journey of David and me with all our precious dogs and fosters.

Elizabeth

Dedication

To all of you who opened up your hearts to rescue a dog. Thank you.

To all the volunteers who work tirelessly with rescue groups. Thank you.

To all our dogs who have sat by my side and sit by me at this moment, bringing joy to my days and contentment as I write. You have touched my heart.

To my husband, David, who has taken this journey with me. I am forever grateful.

I am only one. But still I am one.
I cannot do everything. But still I can do something.
And because I cannot do everything,
I will not refuse to do the something I can do.

Edward Everett Hale

Samson

Soulful eyes fixed on me
Head cocked to one side
Ears up, wishing to understand
Tongue licks my face

Hands squeeze luscious, velvet ears
Follows me everywhere, at my heels
Maneuvering around him, stepping on paw
Sorry, sorry I cry out, hugging him to me

Tail wagging, gentle eyes so bright
Face against his muzzle
Such joy never known
Handsome, Samson boy

Delilah

She melted my heart on sight
The cage caused her such a fright
Her curled-up tail whirled around
And she made such a horrific sound
Oh, please come near
Get me out of here

Her eyes black as coal.
Looking into my very soul
Her constant persistence
Broke down any resistance
In less than an hour
She became ours

No regrets, only joy
      Delightful Delilah

Chapter 1
A Leap of Faith

Dogs have given us their absolute all. We are the center of their universe. We are the focus of their love, faith, and trust. They serve us in return for scraps. It is without a doubt the best deal man has ever made.

Roger A. Caras, Animal Advocate

Our five years with Samson and Delilah in New York City had ended. David retired, and we decided to leave city living and purchase a home with a garden.

After a few months in our new home, I saw an ad for a beagle rescue group in a local paper. I had done adoptions with the San Francisco ASPCA as a volunteer, but this would be different. The rescue group sought volunteers to foster, conduct home visits, and transport dogs to a foster or forever home. What could be more perfect?

Rescuing guarantees that dogs abandoned and tossed aside will not be euthanized in kill shelters or spend weeks, months, and maybe years in a no-kill shelter.

So, there was no doubt that we would always rescue, but how can I get David to agree to foster?

That evening….

"You want us to foster dogs?"

"Why not help other dogs?"

"What about Delilah?"

Of course, we had to consider how Delilah would react to another dog in the family, however temporary. Living in a New York City apartment, we both knew she was afraid of other dogs. She felt trapped in the hallways, trapped in the elevators, and trapped on a lead everywhere we went.

"We won't know about Delilah if we don't try. Someone has to do it? If they don't get fostered, these dogs may lose their lives or end up in a shelter."

"You'll get attached and want to adopt the dog."

"Would that be so bad? I've always wanted four dogs. Besides, they have a rule. You cannot adopt the first dog you foster. It's called a failed foster."

"What about the next dog and the next?"

"We'll see. Let's try one dog and see how it goes."

David shook his head. "I don't see this working. You'll get hurt when you have to give the dog away."

"Let's go in with the mindset that we are doing this to help the dogs. I'm sure that's how others must do it.

"We need to remember we are not to be their destination—their forever home—just part of their journey. If, along the way, we find a dog we want to adopt, then perhaps we'll do it."

"That sounds good in theory."

"It can be in reality. Not every dog we foster should be ours. Some dogs have been denied love, so they should be the only dog and not have to share attention and hugs. We don't know what we're going to get when we foster….

"And just because a dog tears at my heart doesn't mean we should make that dog ours. Besides, Samson and Delilah have to accept them into the pack as well."

The dogs were happier in our new home. When we arrived, Samson and Delilah raced in. They were not sure which room to explore first. Smells were everywhere. We constantly said to each other, "Where are the dogs?" In the apartment in New York City, we never had to wonder—space was at a premium.

The following day I contacted the beagle rescue group. We set up an appointment for a volunteer to meet us and Samson and Delilah. To become a foster home, we had to be screened and approved.

Samson and Delilah were on their best behavior and quickly convinced this beagle lover that they were happy beagles and that we would be a good home for a foster dog.

She smiled and looked at them on the loveseat. "I can't believe they are so well-behaved and quiet."

David and I glanced at each other and smiled.

There was a fenced-in area off the kitchen porch. Delilah amused herself by trying to climb up the magnolia tree in the back garden. The trunk had branched out in different directions.

She got up about four feet, her little legs balancing on the limbs. Such a brave little girl! Her tail was curled up in the air, and her shrill bark sounded a warning to all our neighbors of a squirrel invasion. She was our huntress, while Samson often lazed around like a male lion wherever he could find a sunny spot.

When we were looking for a house, we discovered a lovely beach about twenty minutes away. We took a break from giving the house a facelift, put the dogs in the car, and headed for the water.

When we arrived at the beach, we discovered that dogs were not allowed on the beach beginning in May. I don't understand allowing children and not dogs. It will always be a mystery.

We continued to drive along the coast, hoping to find another area to walk the dogs. Instead, we found a food hut. We stopped to get David an ice cream and maybe a few licks and the cone for the dogs.

I noticed a young woman with a dog heading toward the water and sand. I chased her and called out, "I was told that dogs were not allowed on the beach."

"This is not a state beach. The state beach starts about a mile to the right. You can walk the dogs to the boundary."

With David's ice cream and the dogs in tow, we walked for several hours, enjoying the sun and the waves breaking. We stopped to meet and greet other dogs, and we were never sure if we went beyond the border or not.

On the way back, Samson started digging, sand flying in all directions, trying to find whatever was buried below the surface. We found his antics quite hilarious, and so did passersby who stopped to join in our laughter.

In contrast, Delilah marched along, often letting out a bark at a dog in the distance, sometimes long before we saw it.

We watched with delight as they got close to the water, sniffing at the foaming surf and racing backward when a wave came at them. Once in a while, the dogs were startled by the cold water on their paws. As beagles, they were not water dogs. We didn't have Central Park, but we had this lovely beach.

A few weeks after getting approval to foster, we were asked to foster a three-year-old female beagle named Duchess. We drove to the ASPCA nearby to pick her up. We had not been in a shelter since adopting Samson and Delilah.

This shelter was just as sad as those I remember—rows of cages with dogs, each dog with a longing look, sad eyes, asking for a pet, a kind word, or freedom.

When I saw Duchess behind bars, she looked up with soulful eyes. Oh, those eyes! We were both so upset by the cage and smell that we could not wait to get her out of there.

On the way home, even though she had a strong, unpleasant kennel odor, I cuddled her in a blanket on my lap. I am convinced that bonding between any foster dog and the new foster parents must begin immediately, so I held her in my arms to make her feel safe. David reached over several times to pet her during the thirty-minute journey, and we both spoke words in a soft voice.

Although we didn't know her background, she had been fed, and someone cared for her. Why she was given to the ASPCA was unknown.

We believed that Samson would welcome her with open paws—a playmate. After all, he played with strange dogs in Central Park, and there was never a problem. Delilah had never greeted other dogs with exuberance, so we were not expecting anything different.

On reaching home, we gave Duchess a chance to go on a walkabout in the garden. I brought out Samson and then Delilah to meet her. Having the dogs outside and off the lead and bringing out one at a time would be less threatening to both Duchess and Delilah.

When I went inside to get Samson, my two loves greeted me as though I had been gone for weeks. When they got a whiff of another dog, they knew I had been cheating!

After a sufficient sniff, I brought Samson out to meet Duchess. He did not disappoint. He greeted her with enthusiasm, bouncing around and scooting down on his front paws, his back end in the air, as if saying, "Come on, come on. Play with me."

Duchess did not take him up on his offer. I'm sure she was confused by what was happening, and she was a low-keyed, gentle dog.

The next hurdle was Delilah. She met Duchess nose-to-nose and tails wagging. Then she went off to explore. No drama. That's my sweet Delilah girl.

We had our first foster.

Duchess got a bath, for which I believe she was as grateful as we were. Then the threesome settled in quickly to the routine. Dogs are creatures of habit. They like routine, and Duchess was no exception. She eased into going for walks, roaming outside, and hugs and cuddles.

She did need to be housetrained, and Samson and Delilah helped with that. We praised, applauded, and petted our two when they would tee-tee and doo-doo outside. Duchess would go over and check out why we were so excited. Then she would squat and perform, quickly learning that was one way to get praise, hugs, and pets.

Within a few days, Duchess was housetrained. She understood "respecting the bowl," and all we had to do was give her food and water and make her feel safe. She was content to cuddle around me with Samson and Delilah. As he had done with our original two, David continued the ritual of giving treats after dinner. Again, Duchess was quick to do her part.

A week after Duchess' arrival, I fractured my tibia just below my knee. I fell over a flowerpot that one of our workers had moved. Although it was just a hairline fracture, the cast was heavy and high up on my leg. I could not put my leg down and had to be careful not to fall, breaking off a piece and requiring a pin. That stopped me from getting around quickly and easily. I was in a lot of pain, yet unwilling to take opiates. It was good that life with Duchess was uneventful.

Within three weeks, Duchess was on her way to her forever home. A couple with a young boy had decided to adopt her. The father wanted his son to have a beagle because he had one as a child. A family with a young boy to pet and play with her. Glorious! She would be the "IT" girl, getting all their attention. That is what I had hoped for her.

We drove her south for about an hour. The father and his son immediately hugged her to them and welcomed her with all the joy we wanted for her.

I began to tear up as we drove away. When I finally caught my breath, I said to David, "It's a blessing she was adopted quickly. She didn't have enough time to call our home her home. We didn't have time to fall in forever love with her. Yet, I'm still going to miss her."

"So, do you want to foster again?"

"Yes! It was fun and felt good to help her out."

"But your leg is still in a cast."

That was true. I had been in a lot of pain, and the cast was extremely uncomfortable.

"I'm getting better. We have to continue. There will always be dogs waiting for their turn to be saved."

Chapter 2
Angel and Lady

Abandoned, now loved and cherished
She deserves nothing less
Brow gently caressed

After Duchess was adopted, David presented me with a problem—what to do with the clawfoot tub we had removed from one of the bathrooms so we could put in a shower. The plumber suggested we sell the tub online, but I felt it should stay with this historic home.

"So, where do you want to put it?" David asked, shaking his head.

"Let's put it in our bedroom for now, maybe near the fireplace."

"That's very French—a tub in the bedroom."

I chuckled. "I don't want to bathe in it. Let's put pillows in the bottom so the dogs can sleep in it. That will give us more room in our double bed."

"That's if they'll sleep in it."

Although I enjoyed cuddling the dogs in bed, it would be nice to stretch out our legs. So, we were delighted that Samson and Delilah, without coaxing, jumped in the tub every night. Yet, every morning I called them into our bed and snuggle-buggled until it was time to get up.

A week after Duchess' adoption, we got the call to foster two seven-year-old female dogs, Lady and Angel—

sisters surrendered together, as a result of a divorce. The husband's new lady was allergic to dogs. The wife had to move into an apartment where no dogs were allowed. How sad!

Angel looked part beagle, had arthritis, and was overweight, with a sweet face. Lady looked like there was some spaniel in her and not any beagle. She was bony with eleven teeth missing. The rescue group had vetted both dogs and paid for some major dental work for Lady. A pretty face, she would be regal with a little more weight.

After watching both of them eat their meals, I said to David that Lady was skinny because Angel, the "foody," probably had been eating her sister's food. In the kennel, it was likely no one had been watching. Of course, we watched them both, and "Respect the bowl" was Angel's first lesson.

Again, David included these two fosters in the evening ritual of sitting around him in a semi-circle for treats with Samson and Delilah. David would call out Lady's name, ask her to sit, and give her a treat. If Angel reached for her treat, she would be asked to wait.

We delighted in watching their eyes fixed on David's hand as he reached into the bowl, pulled out a treat, and moved it towards each mouth in turn. Angel and Lady had no difficulty learning the routine.

Although they were well-behaved dogs and loveable, we were not convinced they would get adopted. People searching for a beagle wanted a beagle. Usually, they were seeking a younger dog, often under three years old. Lady was not a beagle, Angel was only part, and both were about seven years old.

At some point we decided that if a foster dog did not get a forever home and time was dragging on, we would keep that dog if Samson and Delilah agreed. At the time, we didn't imagine that we would keep two dogs, but so be it.

Samson played with both girls, although neither was as rambunctious. By now, we knew Delilah was fine with other dogs. "Living off the lead" had made a significant difference in all our lives, and they were all getting along. No skirmishes, just being together.

Because my leg was still in a cast, I had to elevate it and stay off it as much as possible. I then adopted David's recliner as my favorite space to relax since he was out and about doing chores. All four dogs cuddled around me when I collapsed on the recliner.

Usually, it was Samson and Angel on each of the arms of this overstuffed chair, Delilah next to me on the seat, and Lady between my legs on the elevated footstool. Having them snuggled around me brought me so much joy. They also made the tedious hours more contented as I read, wrote, or watched television.

Not all four dogs could fit in the tub comfortably. Angel, with her arthritis and weight, could not jump up anyway. We put a bed between the tub and our bed for the two girls. They snuggled down together, intertwined legs and paws. Both had such gentle manners and were so easy to love.

Within two weeks, we noticed that Angel was losing some of her excess weight. Her new diet and the time outside in the fresh air, racing around, helped. I smiled and remarked to David, "They're happy dogs."

Then one day, about four weeks later, the phone rang, and an adoption counselor told me she had an adopter for Angel and Lady. I was surprised but thought how wonderful for them. We wanted these two sweet girls adopted together.

An arrangement was made for the potential adopter, a single woman, to visit the girls in our home that coming Saturday. When she came through the door, she immediately got on the floor and gathered the dogs around her.

I knew in those first few seconds that they were to be hers. She would be the perfect mom. They would stay together, have this lady, with her generous spirit, as their mom and her undivided attention.

I asked her why she had decided to adopt a dog. "Both of my boys are no longer with me. My youngest just joined the Army. I'm all alone."

"Why did you decide on these two?"

"Well, I was going to adopt another dog on your site, but it took so long to get her out of another state. Then, I saw these two, and I just knew I wanted two."

I explained about Angel's arthritis and Lady's teeth. She listened but did not balk at facing their health problems. As she wrote out a check for the adoption fee, she said, "I wish I could give you more. I know these two have been a great expense for your group."

"Not to worry. We're grateful you're taking both of the girls."

After a pleasant visit and a chance for her to relax, she was on her way home with our two-not-to-be doggies.

After this adoption, I contacted the Adoption Director. I suggested that we give a special price to anyone who adopted two dogs, not only to encourage them to do so but to give them a financial break.

The following day I got an e-mail from Angel and Lady's new mom thanking me for fostering them and letting me know she had bought a set of stairs so Angel could get into bed with her and Lady, plus some soft treats for Lady. I smiled, happy to know they would be cared for with compassion.

We had made the right decision—letting them go. We were a family of four once again.

Chapter 3
Sissy and Snoopy

Toys tossed in the air
Racetrack in the fluffy snow
Joy for all to know

Because we were keen to foster twosomes, along came another pair—Sissy and Snoopy. When I first saw Sissy, I noticed that she had only one eye. Her other eye—well, it looked like it had shriveled up.

Both dogs were tri-colored, though Snoopy had a rich black color over most of his stout body, bright dark eyes, and a love-bug personality.

When they arrived at the house, we did the usual introduction, and immediately Sissy and Samson started racing around at hyper speed. Our Samson boy had a playmate.

When we took Sissy and Snoopy to our vet to remove their spaying and neutering stitches, I asked about Sissy's eye. Our vet, Dr. H, told us that her eye had shriveled up.

"Why would that happen?" I asked.

"I'm not sure—maybe an infection, or maybe she was born that way."

We believe for everyone who wants an arm-candy dog, there are people with compassionate hearts who would adopt a dog like Sissy. I was also keen to watch the dynamics with Delilah, just in case.

We both knew the fosters, like our two, would get noticed and petted by people when we walked them around the neighborhood and into town. It also gave us a chance to tell their story and explain that they needed a home. Now that I was walking again, we could take them out and about.

Once someone heard they were foster dogs, an obvious comment was, "I could never foster. I could never give them up. How can you do that?"

Of course, knowing this might happen, I had already thought about my response, so I would say, "If we don't foster, who will? If we don't foster, what would happen to these dogs? Someone has to step up."

Then I would pause to let those thoughts sink in. "If they go to a shelter, they will not learn how to live in a home, experience hugs and pets, and be socialized. Then when they are adopted, they might be returned because they are still on square one.

"Fostering gives these dogs a better chance of an adoption sticking. What would you choose, a home where you are given attention or a cage in a shelter?" Whew! That felt good!

Still, the reply that came back, "But how can you give them up?"

"Because we realize that not every dog should be our dog. Every dog needs a different situation. We also keep in mind that we are to be part of each foster's journey, not the final destination, and that's OK.

"Yes, one day, we may keep one, but it will be because our dogs have bonded with that dog, or it's time for us to add to the pack or...."

My soap box was in high gear.

"But don't you want to keep them?" was often a reply.

"We start by protecting our hearts. We are forever mindful that the foster is not ours. We take care of them, pet and fuss over them, and train them in the basics."

I sighed. "Also, when you foster, you realize in time that not all dogs should be with you forever. You also realize that it is kinder to let them go. That may be difficult to understand, but it can be a reality."

I may not have convinced them to foster that very day. Maybe they still walked away wondering how we could give a foster away, but then maybe I gave them something to consider in the future. Rescue groups need foster homes.

This twosome would be with us for the holidays, so I put Christmas bells on their collars as I did with Samson and Delilah. David's daughter, her three children, her partner, and his two children would be coming from England for the holidays.

When David told his daughter we had four dogs, she commented, "Can't you find another one? I'm coming with five children." We laughed because we knew that could be a possibility.

When the family arrived, the children were thrilled to find four dogs greeting them with tail wags and kisses. Then they noticed the stockings hung on the mantel over the fireplace in the kitchen—thirteen in all. There were four for the dogs and the other nine for the adults and children. They delighted in finding their stockings and guessing which stocking was for each of the dogs.

A couple of nights later, I let the dogs outside before going to bed. The house was hectic so I forgot our rule of going outside with the dogs, but then they never seemed interested in leaving the yard. Besides, it was all fenced in. Samson and Delilah came running when I called out, but Sissy and Snoopy did not.

I stepped out into the driveway and felt the cold wind on my face. I looked towards the gate and could see in the moonlight that it was swaying back and forth. The latch on the gate had been released, giving Sissy and Snoopy freedom.

I ran into the house and yelled, "Sissy and Snoopy have gotten out of the yard. We have to find them."

My heart was pounding at the thought of not finding these dogs in the pitch-black December night. Within seconds, the kids had put on their coats and shoes and were out the door.

David got the car and started driving around the neighboring streets. I stayed home in case David called, saying he had found one or both. The kids returned a few minutes later with Sissy and Snoopy in their arms.

"How did you find them? Where did you find them?" I shouted.

The thirteen-year-old girl yelled, "Across the street in that yard," pointing to the house directly across from ours.

Christopher, the sixteen-year-old grandson, added, "We heard the Christmas bells around their necks. That's how we found them."

I smiled, remembering that was how I always knew where Samson was in our New York apartment. That night David said he would get a heavier latch for the gate. We pledged again that we would never leave the dogs out of the house without one of us and always check the gate before we opened the door.

Whew! That was just too scary!

The family left to return to England the day after Christmas. We then hosted a Christmas party for neighbors and friends. Of course, the dogs were the entertainment, not because they chose to be, but because they were so cute.

I don't think I'm partial, but it is impossible to resist a beagle. Someone asked about the challenges of walking four dogs. We hadn't found it challenging. But another suggested a double lead—a short piece of rope with a clip at each end for two dogs and a connecter in the center for the lead.

David gave it a go and made two, thinking one lead might be easier to hold and manage than two. We connected Snoopy and Delilah on one lead because their pace was less frantic, and Samson and Sissy shared the other. We had quite a few laughs as we watched Samson or Sissy pulling the other in the direction they wanted to go, but neither seemed to mind.

We soon realized we had another challenge. There were way too many rooms for the dogs to wander, so we started doing a headcount of the dogs, finding it difficult to keep track of Sissy and Samson. Often, when we were on the move, we noticed that a dog or two was missing. Then one of us had to go in search.

We decided that I, the "pied-piper," as David had nicknamed me, would go first, calling the dogs. David would hang back and then say, "How many do you have?"

"I've got two."

"I've got one."

"OK, who's missing."

This was a ritual every morning when we came down the stairs, when we would go outside or come into the house, and when we retired at night. It made us laugh and reassured us that all were accounted for.

About a week into the new year, there was a family with a son and daughter who wanted to adopt Sissy.

I questioned the adoption counselor, "Sissy? An adopter for Sissy? What about Snoopy?"

"No, they just want Sissy."

"Don't you think we should try to keep them together?"

"It's difficult to get someone to take two dogs. They have two children and are anxious to meet Sissy. They're willing to drive to your house to meet her."

A day later I spoke with the children's mother and set up a day for a visit. We were mindful to keep Samson and Delilah squirreled away. We didn't want them to overshadow the dog they wanted to adopt. But I wanted them to meet Snoopy, fall in love, and adopt him as well.

He was such a darling boy, and I believed they should be kept together. They played nicely and snuggled together at night. Neither was bossy or dominated the other, which is important in a twosome.

On the designated Saturday, a couple with a boy and girl—around ten and twelve—appeared at the front door.

Sissy and Snoopy greeted them as though they had known them for years. That was the first step.

We spent the next hour talking about this and that and the dogs. They were lovely people, and their children were so well behaved. All were dog lovers.

Finally, I asked that all-important question, "Why don't you adopt both dogs? You have two children. They will probably end up fighting over one dog. With two dogs, you won't have that problem."

Then I gave them my "two dogs are easier than one" speech. "When we were going to adopt a dog, I told David that we had to adopt two. I have had two, and I have had one, and two dogs are so much easier."

"Are they really?" said the mother.

I chuckled, "I think so. Two dogs play together, sleep together, and clean each other's ears.... Besides, most dogs are pack animals, and I once heard that beagles are the #1 pack animal. They want to have a companion, especially when you're not around. There are circumstances when a dog should be the only dog, but this isn't one of them."

I was disappointed when they told me they would need to talk about it and left without either dog. I wondered if I had lost Sissy the chance to be adopted by pushing the idea of Snoopy. Maybe they felt they should stay together too. In the end, I decided what was supposed to be would be.

Later that day, I got a call from the mother. "We've decided to adopt both dogs."

I almost screamed with delight but stopped myself so she could continue. "We just had to see how our son would react to dog hair. He has allergies, and we weren't sure if the dog hair would bother him. It did not, and we agree with you. We should have the two dogs."

I was always in two minds when our fosters got adopted. I wanted them to find a forever home. I also told myself day after day while they were with us that they were just visiting. We signed up for a short time. We were the transition family.

The following day we met the family who was thrilled to welcome two dogs into their lives, and we were happy for them.

Once again, our original two had our undivided attention, and both pairs we fostered were kept together. Such bliss!

Chapter 4
Jake and Zoey

No one appreciates the very special genius of your conversation as much as the dog does.
Christopher Morley

It was spring again, and Delilah, our huntress, was on the prowl for squirrels. They taunted her by running along the top of the fence, and she did not disappoint as she chased after them and barked.

One night we returned late from dinner at a local restaurant. We quickly let the dogs out for their evening ritual. While David kept an eye on the dogs, I ran upstairs to change. Suddenly, I heard barking and howling and then David yelling, "Elizabeth, Elizabeth."

I ran downstairs, still dressed. I heard a shrill bark from Delilah. She was in full voice, and Samson was howling, running around.

When David saw me on the porch, he yelled, "Delilah cornered a skunk. She's not going to back down. Stay there!"

Finally, David appeared out of the dark, holding Delilah out in front of him—the smell of skunk filling the air.

"Oh, my heaven. She got sprayed. How's Samson?"

"I think he's OK. I think he is more afraid than anything. It's Delilah who took on the skunk."

I looked around and found Samson on the porch. Our brave boy!

"I'll take her up and put her in the tub. Get me some cans of tomatoes and tomato sauce from the larder."

"Do you think that will work?"

"I don't have a clue."

I put Delilah in the tub, took off my shawl, and stepped out of my dress. David arrived with the tomatoes and the juice. We poured that all over Delilah's head and neck, trying to avoid her eyes.

She had taken the full blast in the face. She looked like a drowned beagle with red goop all over her. After massaging the tomatoes into her fur for about fifteen minutes, we bathed her, toweled her off, and threw the towels in the washer.

Once Delilah was dry, we realized that the tomatoes had not removed all the smell, although it was somewhat better. We gave her one more bath, adding baking soda, hoping, but our hopes were dashed. Samson also got a bath just because we discovered he had a skunk odor, too, although slight.

They slept in our bedroom that night, but a slight odor from Delilah permeated the air. We bathed her again the next day. That skunk had sprayed her directly in the face. I did not want to irritate her eyes, so I had difficulty washing her face. She was patient with me, accepting her fate, but that was sweet Delilah.

Her eyes were red, and she was throwing up a yellow liquid. We decided that the skunk spray got into her nose and mouth and then drained into her stomach.

The next day I bathed her face in white vinegar, which helped some, and another bath with Dawn liquid, peroxide, and baking soda. Over the next few days, I kept smelling skunk in our bedroom. I washed the bed linen and kept checking for what might be causing the odor.

On the third day, I opened the drawer where I kept my shawls and scarves, and the odor almost threw me across the room. That's where the smell was coming from. The shawl I had on that night had become drenched in the skunk smell. I took everything out of the drawer and washed it, and I washed the drawer with soap, baking soda, and water several times.

Our little Delilah had shown herself to be the huntress and protector we always thought she was. Now, we knew we were safe not only from squirrels but skunks as well. Unfortunately, it was a week before the skunk odor was completely gone. We were grateful.

When we got the call to foster Jake and Zoey, we realized, in some ways, it was a blessing not knowing our foster's history. So many sad stories. Jake and Zoey's human companion was in the Army Reserves. His unit had been called up, and he had been deployed.

He had asked his parents to take care of his two dogs for the year he would be away. The parents had kept the dogs outside. No doggie comforts.

The son then called almost a year later to tell his parents that his tour had been extended for another eight months. They decided they would no longer care for his dogs and contacted the rescue group.

When we picked up these three-year-old dogs, Jake, the male, had on an Elizabethan collar. He was stocky, with a wide-track stance, and low to the ground with very long, floppy ears. Zoey was about eight pounds lighter and small-boned. They had just been neutered and spayed.

Although there was no joyous, spontaneous greeting between our dogs and these two fosters, the initial meeting happened without any incident. Jake and Zoey were not interested in any kind of play with Samson, and both of our dogs stayed away from Jake. Maybe the Elizabethan collar was a turnoff.

We thought that Jake's collar was to keep him from biting his stitches. When I removed it, I realized that the collar was to stop him from biting his belly, paws, and any other body part he could reach.

It was spring, so Jake spent most of his day on the porch trying to dig at his paws and belly even though the collar was to stop him. How could I help him, I asked myself every day? I decided hot spots might be causing him to bite himself. Maybe the area he came from was infested with fleas. It could be a flea allergy.

I went to a pet store and bought some ointment I used years ago for my beagle Boomer whom I had rescued off the street. I applied it several times daily, but the salve did not stop Jake from chewing at his paws. I spoke with someone in our rescue group, and we discussed the possibility that his need to chew was nerves. He had been through such an ordeal. Some dogs are resilient; others are not.

Zoey was the opposite of Jake, not only in looks but in temperament. She was calm and gentle and seemed to be saying with her eyes, "If I have to live here, let's be friends."

Because we always wanted the foster dogs to feel part of the pack, they came into our sitting room at night and cuddled on their dog beds.

One night, David sat down on his favorite chair, and Jake jumped on his lap. We were delighted. It was the first sign of his feeling safe and comfortable and wanting to be with us. By this time, Jake had settled in and had stopped chewing his paws.

Up until then, he had shown no interest in the other three dogs or us, so this came as a welcome surprise. Maybe he remembered his former life. Maybe he remembered his master lost to him now forever. Maybe because he was raised by a man, David could help with his settling in.

Then Zoey came near, and he growled at her. Delilah came near, and he lunged at her. That concerned us, but we hoped it would work out in time.

Then a few nights later, we were in our bedroom, and Jake surprised me by jumping on the bed. As I was petting him and cooing in his ear, Samson jumped up to get some loving. "Me too, me too."

Jake attacked him, snarling and biting. Samson tried to get away, but it was too late. I saw blood oozing from Samson's front paws.

I called to David, and he came running and grabbed Jake, getting nipped for his efforts.

"Take him downstairs and put him in a crate," I shouted.

Fortunately, someone in the rescue group had offered us, as new fosters, a crate. We took it just in case there was ever a need. This was that need.

I swept Samson in my arms and ran to the bathroom. After wiping away the blood, I could see the injury was minor—just one small hole in each paw. I smiled, remembering when he got bit by a rat in Central Park.

Later, I took Samson downstairs to test the waters with Jake. Samson would be safe because Jake was still in the crate. Jake started clawing at the bars and growling, trying to get at Samson.

This happened again the next day. We had to take Jake and the other dogs out separately, and we had to keep Jake crated. It was too scary not to do so. It was as though something inside him had snapped.

We did not believe he was a bad dog. We did know that there had been little human contact for a whole year, so he felt abandoned and confused for so long. No way to explain to him what was happening. It was heartbreaking.

After two days, it was clear we had to have Jake evaluated. The evaluation revealed he was not dangerous to people, and as we had suspected, he was a troubled dog who needed a foster home and then adopters who had no other dogs.

We continued to foster Zoey and later learned Jake was fostered by a couple who did not have a dog and later they adopted him. The foster parents saved a beating heart, and I am forever grateful for their compassion and generosity of spirit.

Chapter 5
Happy Ending for Zoey

Before you get a dog, you can't quite imagine what living with one might be like; afterward, you can't imagine living any other way.
                              Caroline Knapp

We had fostered eight dogs in ten months. After fostering Duchess, it never occurred to us to stop. Opening our lives to these rescue dogs was one of the most fulfilling things we had done in this world—not only for them but for the two of us.

A few weeks after Jake left our home, we learned that a couple who had two boys wanted to adopt Zoey. During my discussion with the mother of the twosome, I learned Zoey would be their first dog. We set up a time for them to visit that weekend.

"So, what do you think? Do they seem to be the right people for Zoey?" said David.

"I'm not sure. Let's face it. So far, I believe our fosters got great homes."

After greeting the family, I handed each of them a treat to give to Zoey when they met her. Since Zoey was so shy, it would give them a way to connect with her and make Zoey more comfortable.

Once the four were in the living room, David brought Zoey in. The father and older boy, who was about eight, greeted her with pets and sweet words. I suggested that they ask her to sit before giving her the treat. Zoey complied, and the two of them petted her again and again.

The younger boy was clinging to his mother's side as we talked about Zoey's general behavior. Finally, I suggested that we take Zoey outside where the boys could play with her.

The father and the older boy headed out into the yard with David. They played with Zoey while the mother stood in the kitchen. The younger boy was still by her side. I suggested that we go out to the porch to watch Zoey's playful antics, but she stood firm and did not move.

My patience was failing me. I wanted to see some indication that she liked dogs. She wasn't buying an appliance.

"So, what do you think of Zoey?"

"Well, I don't know. We haven't bonded."

Bonded!!!! I must admit I wanted to do bodily harm. Instead, I said as calmly as I could, "What have you done to bond with her? The treats I gave you and your son are still in your hands. Your husband and your other son gave her the treats and are now playing with her. If you look outside, you would see what a great dog she is."

That was it. Patience gone. I took a breath.

"How do you expect her to bond with you? You haven't paid her any attention. She's the dog. You're the human. That's your responsibility. She's been through an ordeal. She's not a pushy dog. If you would have just given her some attention, called her to you...."

I guess she was shocked by my response, and I must admit so was I. Yes, we wanted Zoey to start living her life in a forever home, protected, loved, and secure, but this woman was like an ice cube, and somehow, she had passed on her way of moving in the world to her son.

Maybe she was afraid of dogs, or she didn't want a dog. Maybe this was an exercise to remove the pressure from her husband and older son who wanted a dog. They would never get that dog if she kept finding fault.

She called to her husband and son. I walked them to the door, and the husband and I chatted. I felt sorry for him and the older son. The two would have been great adopters, but you don't adopt a dog to half a family. You don't give a dog to someone who finds faults when there are none.

As I said goodbye, I did not say, "Call me if you have any questions." Instead, I wished them a safe journey home and raced inside to hug Zoey.

"Well, they're not going to get Zoey, even if her husband changes her mind," I said to David.

"So, what are you going to do?"

"Well, I have to tell the adoption counselor what happened. It's a touchy situation. They have been approved as adopters."

David knelt and petted Zoey. "Yes, but those who approved them didn't see what we saw. She ignored Zoey and treated her as if she were not there."

Tears welled in my eyes, "I could not believe that she was so cold to Zoey. Her husband was the opposite. I would have agreed to adopt the dog to him, but not her."

"So, you've got to tell the counselor."

"I know. Zoey is just too precious. I want her in a home where she will receive love and hugs and pets."

"Well, we could keep her. She gets that here."

"Maybe that will happen, but maybe it would be better for her to be the only dog. She has had such a tough time."

I sent an e-mail to the adoption counselor telling her that I was convinced this adopter should not have any of our dogs, especially Zoey.

Her reply, "How do I tell her that?"

She was a new adoption counselor, and I could tell she was hesitant to nix an adopter.

"Give me a few minutes to put something together, and I'll e-mail it to you."

I spent the next ten minutes crafting a message that she might be able to deliver. The gist was, "Our dogs are in many towns and cities, many miles apart in foster homes. You cannot keep driving from place to place, trying to find the perfect dog with our rescue group. There are many shelters near your home, so we suggest you try there."

Deep down, I believed no dog would be perfect enough for her. In the end, Zoey might be returned. I was unwilling to risk it.

Zoey continued to live with us, and all our days with her were peaceful, feel-good days. She was similar to Delilah in energy and contentment. Often, I found the two of them snuggling on one bed together, or they would cuddle with me on a chair.

A few weeks after this incident, I got another call. Adopters were interested in Zoey, especially the wife. She explained that their dog had passed away, and she was lonesome for another one.

Her husband was not as keen because he had been recently diagnosed with a degenerative disease. He was not sure he would have the energy for a dog. His wife hoped he would fall for Zoey and forget his concerns. Because Zoey was so quiet and loving, it could be an excellent situation for all.

When they came through the door, it was love at first sight—for both of them. I'm not exaggerating when I recall that it took less than ten seconds. The husband's eyes lit up. Ten years lifted from his face. The wife fussed over Zoey, petting her and cooing about how sweet she was. Someone who appreciated the wonderfulness of Zoey.

Neither of them could believe she was so pretty and so gentle. They were besotted. They visited for a while, hearing stories about Zoey, asking about her favorite food, the treats she craved, and the toys she liked.

Before they left, the husband insisted on taking a picture of me with his wife and Zoey. I then took a picture of the two of them with Zoey. I can still see the wife hugging their precious cargo and the joy on both of their faces as they waved goodbye.

Zoey was meant for this family. Not only would Zoey's life be enriched, but so would theirs. This gentle dog was going to be loved and cared for. In return, she was going to take away some sadness in the lives of her guardians. Now they would have a purpose—to care for a dog who had experienced a tough year and the loss of her master and her companion.

Chapter 6
Annie, Thelma, and Louise

Dogs laugh, but they laugh with their tails.
Max Eastman

Annie, our next foster, was a gentle five-year-old, thirteen-inch beagle, and resembled sweet Zoey. She came to us perfect and left our home as quickly as she came. A young man had graduated from college and would be moving away from home, leaving his mother alone. His concern for her prompted him to adopt a dog to give her for Mother's Day, and he chose Annie.

There was somewhat of a risk because it would surprise his mother, something she wasn't expecting. What if she didn't like Annie, but who wouldn't fall in love with Annie? The adoption counselor believed it was a match. Since the young man was so keen, we drove Annie south over one hundred miles to meet him.

When we arrived, he greeted Annie with much enthusiasm. If his mom were anything like him, Annie would not be returned. His mother had raised a loving, kind son.

On Mother's Day, I received a call from his mother telling me how special and lovely Annie was and thanking me for being such a great foster Mom.

A footnote: She called the following year on Mother's Day, again praising Annie and my efforts on Annie's behalf. We were delighted we had been part of Annie's journey and that her forever guardian was so loving and thankful for her.

About a month after Annie's adoption, we were asked to foster another twosome—two female dogs, Thelma and Louise.

Thelma had a delicate face with soft brown eyes and was tri-color. Louise had a broad face with long ears that hung past her chin. She was a dark rusty brown and black. Her paws were chubby, and I was immediately drawn to her. There was something about her eyes—sadness mixed with fear.

The ride home was long and tedious, but the girls finally settled in and fell asleep. Louise snuggled next to me. Samson and then Delilah welcomed them when we arrived home. Within seconds, Thelma and Samson were racing around the yard. Louise, we soon discovered, was very skittish and afraid, especially of David.

Louise started packing around the yard. I sat down, hoping she would come to me. She approached within a few feet and then backed away. She did this again and again. Then about a half-hour later, she came to me and rested her head on my lap. When a dog does that, you are hooked!

David shook his head. "How are we ever going to get her in the house?"

"We'll figure it out."

Of course, I could have caught her and put a lead on and dragged her in, but in reality, she needed to come in on her own. Dragging her would frighten her more.

Holding out a treat was of no interest. She would not come into the house if she could see either of us. I hid behind the door, and once she entered—sometimes after too-many minutes—I would close the door, trapping her inside. Then she would scamper to a corner where she hoped she would not be seen.

By the end of the day, she would come to me now and then, and I could pet her. Samson had kept Thelma entertained, racing around and making sure she was exhausted by the end of the day.

Over the next week, I made some progress with Louise, but David had not. Because he was so busy with chores outside the house, he could not give her the time and attention she needed to trust him and not be afraid. When she wasn't near Delilah and me, she stayed close to Thelma, who ignored her most of the time.

One of the reasons we agreed to foster siblings was the belief they should be given a chance to stay together, if at all possible. However, we soon wondered if that were true for Thelma and Louise.

Louise was too skittish to be adopted. She needed socialization and time, effort, and patience from us. If we separated them, Thelma might get adopted within weeks. Not only was she a good-looking beagle, but in addition to her rambunctious behavior, she had endearing qualities.

David and I also thought it would be good to get Louise out of the shadow of Thelma. We had to consider what was best for these two little girls. We became convinced they needed a different kind of home and human companion.

Louise would be best as an only dog in a quiet home with someone who wanted a quiet, gentle dog and who would have patience. Thelma would be best with a playmate or adopters who would give her lots of walks and playtime.

🐾

About a week later, I woke up one morning and was bent over in pain. The pain in my upper back made it impossible for me to move more than a few feet. After a visit to the doctor, I was put on bed rest.

We decided that since moving about was so painful, I would stay in a bedroom at the top of the stairs. It would be a shorter distance for David to bring me my meals.

After a few days, David came into the bedroom with my lunch. I could see the frustration on his face.

"Elizabeth, I can't do this anymore. It's just too much. Louise won't come to me, and she won't come in. Thelma races around and won't come in either. It's just too much."

What could I say? David not only had to make the meals and bring them to me, but he also had four dogs to take care of—one that would not come to him for food or pets and would not come in at night.

We both knew I had a sweet spot in my heart for Louise. Part of my sympathy for her was imagining what it was like to live in constant fear. I had made progress with her, but now I could not spend the time with her she needed. It was clear she and I had run out of time together.

I spoke with the Foster Director, and within a few days, Thelma and Louise were sent to another foster home. Within a week, we heard that Thelma was adopted and then a few weeks later, Louise too.

I could not believe Louise was adopted. I just hoped whoever adopted her would be willing to put in the necessary time and energy to help her trust and feel secure.

A week later, Louise was back on the rescue website, having been returned by her adopters. A few weeks later, she was adopted again, and again she was returned. It was then I called the Adoption Director for some information.

"Well, the last man who adopted her was adding to his pack. He wanted a pure beagle and said she wasn't."

"But she's a gorgeous dog. Maybe because she is two colors and has big paws, she might have some other breed in her. Didn't the guy know that before taking her? Wouldn't the foster family know that? Did he ask?"

"I didn't know that, so I guess he didn't either. It was never mentioned that he wanted a pure-bred dog."

"She's a troubled dog and needs someone with understanding. He definitely wasn't that person."

"I have another adopter. She is more than willing to work with her."

I sighed, "Dear Louise. She's such a beautiful dog. Please call me if this adoption doesn't stick. We'll adopt her. I don't want her to go through this again."

By this time, I was well again, and I knew I could keep that promise. Yet, deep down, I believed Louise should be the only dog. She needed so much attention, but I didn't want her to be returned again. I never got that call, and she never reappeared on the website. But she had taken a piece of my heart with her.

Chapter 7

Dear Sweet Bonnie

Follows me everywhere
Priceless for the joy she brings
For my laughter that rings out

It was late September when we got a call to foster a female dog from a puppy mill.

A rescue group in a Midwest state had bought a three-year old blue-tick beagle from the auction block. They did that so another breeder could not buy her. To continue her journey, they needed a rescue group with foster homes.

She would need about two months of tender, loving care before she could be spayed, having birthed who-knows-how-many puppies every time she came in heat.

Puppy-mill dogs do not come with a name. Why name them? They would never be called to be petted or hugged and cuddled, never called to walk on a lead. Instead, a number was stamped in their ears to identify them. The name she had been given by the rescue group was Bonnie.

The volunteer who had transported Bonnie spoke only a few words as she handed me the lead—sadness filling the air that no words could erase. Bonnie had a lovely broad face and long ears, so long they almost touched the ground. As she came toward us, we could see that she was moving slowly, hobbling along, and there was no wagging tail.

Her belly skin had been stretched and was hanging down, like her ears, maybe two inches from the ground. Her legs were bowed in, and it was clear it was difficult for her to walk.

Visibly, we could see Bonnie was a crippled dog, but what lurked within her we still had to learn. Anger coursed through my body that the government and society permit irresponsible breeding and puppy mills.

David picked up Bonnie and placed her on the pillow on my lap. Both of us had tears in our eyes. As I sat there holding her and rubbing her ears, she looked around with her soft brown eyes, seeming to say, "That feels good."

I hugged her to me as we rode home, and David continually reached over to stroke her head. We both talked to her softly.

When we arrived, Samson did not greet her with his usual exuberance, nor did he try to get her to play. After a few sniffs, Delilah went to her bed. I called Bonnie over to join her, and they snuggled down together. While I made dinner, David and I petted her between chores and tried to make her feel comfortable.

Of course, Bonnie had never been given any exercise and had never been allowed any kind of everyday dog life. The confines of the cage she had lived in for three years had weakened her legs.

She was overweight, not because she had been well-fed, but because they had fed her food that would keep weight on her so she could breed. Profit being the only motive, there was no reason to give her food that would keep her healthy and no profit to be made by doing so.

When we agreed to foster Bonnie, we knew very little about puppy mills, except we wanted them outlawed. While talking with the volunteer from the group who bought her from the auction block, I learned that many puppy mills and breeders usually breed female dogs for three years and then turn them out.

During the first three years of her life, a female dog usually gives birth to large litters, often over ten or more puppies at a time. Also, during that time, female dogs come into heat at least every six months, giving birth every time. No break in between.

At three years, a female dog does not come in heat as often, and the litters become smaller, reducing the profits for the puppy mills. Health problems also increase, so veterinary care costs would increase, if indeed they cared for the female dogs.

The solution is to replace a three-year-old dog with a young female. Then the older females are sold directly to an individual breeder or put into an auction. Then, anyone can buy those females and still breed them.

The female dogs are just a resource to be used repeatedly and then discarded.

After eating a yummy dinner with cooked chicken and vegetables, Bonnie took a short nap. Later, David carried her outside to a place where she could perform without walking too far. This was a new experience for her. She was accustomed to a cage and wire and cement.

We decided to let her walk halfway back to the house. Somehow her legs had to get stronger, and we had to try and balance the need for her to exercise with the concern that walking was painful for her.

The USDA uses a formula to determine the minimum cage size for each dog at a USDA-licensed facility, meaning a puppy mill. To meet Animal Welfare Act standards, all dogs, no matter what breed or size, must have a cage size that is six inches wider and six inches longer than the width and length of the dog. Imagine! Just six inches! What callous people make these laws?

To add to this inhumane standard, the dogs are allowed to spend their entire life that way. No running, no jumping, no playing, no comforts, no long walks, no touches, no love, and no steps to walk up and down. Imagine!

All five of us went into our library that evening, and I called Bonnie to a soft bed. These comforts were new to her, but she welcomed all the attention she was given, getting closer and closer to me when I petted her.

Her legs were not strong enough to go up any steps, nor did she know how to take one step at a time to make her way up. Puppy mill dogs, like laboratory dogs, are not familiar with going up steps, so they have to learn. It's not as automatic as one might think.

That night was the first of many that David carried Bonnie up to the second floor to sleep with all of us. The following morning, David carried her downstairs. Both of us felt such sorrow, watching how weak she was. Sweet Bonnie was breaking both our hearts.

She was loving and gentle. She just wanted to be near us and Samson and Delilah. It was amazing how quickly she settled in and how she responded to the smallest kindnesses.

After a few days, she came up to me one evening, wrapped her front paws around one of my legs and held on tight. Tears welled up in our eyes, and I started sobbing. I knelt down, wrapped her in my arms, and spoke to her in a soft voice. Bonnie so desperately wanted the human touch—all the kindnesses she had been denied for those three years.

We became so angry about this pernicious business of puppy mills that we spoke to anyone who would listen about not buying puppies from pet stores or breeders. We were then, and still today, determined to encourage everyone to rescue a dog from a shelter or volunteer rescue organizations, where all donations and money raised are used for the welfare of the dogs.

If the demand for puppies decreases, the supply will decrease. That way, we hope this will reduce the number of dogs like Bonnie, crippled by the greed of insensitive puppy-mill owners and breeders.

With tears in my eyes as I sat hugging Bonnie, I said to David, "I wonder how many people know that the dog they are buying in that pet store or from a breeder may be birthed under such horrible conditions—that the mother of that puppy has suffered so.

"It's not like years ago when people bred a dog now and then—and sold or even gave away the puppies. Now it's a rotten, cruel, callous business, but how can we stop this?"

We decided to spread the word. Friends were accustomed to coming to our home and hearing about the plight of dogs. When visitors stopped by, we told Bonnie's story at length. We did it, hoping we could encourage people to rescue a dog and encourage their friends to do the same.

Our hearts ached as we watched this beautiful dog try to walk. We spoke about how could anybody treat any dog in such a brutal and cold-hearted way.

I answered, "Why do a day's work when you can have a defenseless dog earn money for you?" And I don't apologize for those thoughts.

To add to our concerns about her physical disabilities, Bonnie's socialization had been nil, living in a small cage with minimal human contact.

After a couple of weeks of our routine and home, we started walking her short distances with Samson and Delilah. That would help get her legs stronger and give her a chance to meet other dogs and people.

Having been so deprived of human contact, she loved the attention of strangers and melted into the arms of anyone who stopped to pet her. Within several weeks, she was marching beside our two, her legs getting stronger every day and the excess pounds coming off. All three were a happy trio.

After several weeks, Bonnie began to negotiate the two steps from the mudroom to the kitchen. Still, we noticed she was hesitant when she looked at the flight of steps to the second floor. That's where Samson and Delilah helped out. Once her legs became strong enough, she started going up the steps without any coaxing on our part, following the other two. She was still not willing to come down.

About a week later, she started coming down the steps. We celebrated. But even more endearing, she started jumping on our laps when we sat in a recliner. She wanted some of what Samson and Delilah were getting, cuddling next to us on a comfy chair and our undivided attention, even though we gave her plenty of pets and hugs.

We were coming up on two months with Bonnie in our home, and it was time to get her spayed. Over those months, she had lost weight, and her legs were stronger. She pranced around the house with renewed energy. She also followed one of us, especially me, everywhere.

The pied-piper name David had given me years ago was more evident with Bonnie than any other foster dog. Some might have called her clingy, but I did not mind her being by my side, often with Samson, 24/7.

There was also something else that made my heart soar. One day I walked into the dining room and saw her toss one of Samson's toys in the air.

When Bonnie first came to us, she showed no interest, had no idea what a toy was. Now, she was throwing a teddy bear up in the air and chewing it to pieces. She had come full circle—from being a dog in looks ONLY to being a happy, playful dog.

Chapter 8
Puppy Mills and Breeders

If you don't believe dogs have souls, you haven't looked into their eyes long enough.
Unknown

During our time with Bonnie, the rescue group was called upon to take in fourteen dogs. Eighteen adult dogs were taken from inside a home after the owner had passed away. All were beagles of some variety, some pregnant. Our group took thirteen of the dogs, plus another hound roaming outside. The local ASPCA took the other dogs.

All of them needed to be spayed or neutered. The pregnant females needed to go to a home where the foster parents could take care of a pregnant dog and help wean the puppies. The dogs and the puppies would need all their shots. The veterinary costs would be outrageous.

The appeal went out for fundraisers and donations, as well as for foster homes. With Bonnie's history spinning in my head and heart and now hearing of this situation, I wrote an article for the local newspaper. I explained the life puppy-mill dogs endure and the work that rescue groups do, highlighting the story of Bonnie.

There's a saying that events come in threes, and this third one compelled me to take further action. There was an article in the newspaper about a man who owned a puppy mill with over ninety dogs. He was taken to court on several violations, fined $2,500, and the dogs removed. $2,500!!

Apparently, the writer of the article, having zero understanding of such situations, said that the reason for the ENORMOUS (the writer's word) fine was to pay for the veterinary bills for the dogs at the mill.

I shared the story with David, "That reporter and that judge know nothing about veterinary costs! $2,500 wouldn't pay for ten dogs, let alone over ninety, to be spayed, neutered, vaccinated, and vetted. And who ends up paying for irresponsible breeding? Why don't they do something about these puppy mills and unscrupulous breeders?"

David shook his head. "What would you have done if you were in charge?"

"First, I would have vetted all the dogs and made him pay the entire bill. Second, I would not allow him to start another puppy mill or any business that involved breeding dogs. I would have no mercy. Not only was that fine ridiculous, but he also needs to be made to suffer as he made those dogs suffer."

Soon after those events, I became aware of legislation at the State level. A state representative had written legislation defining what was meant by a breeder. I contacted him to support his efforts. He told me that he had already received several bullying calls and threats from angry constituents about his proposal. He seemed shaken and was delighted to have some support.

"What's wrong with defining who would be considered a breeder?"

"I don't know. My bill states that anyone with more than five females not spayed is considered a breeder. You can check it out online. Would you be willing to appear at the hearings and give testimony in favor of the legislation?"

I agreed that we would be there, so David and I made the trip to the state capitol. Every chair in the room was filled. People were standing around the walls as well. We heard testimony for and against the bill for over three hours.

From the people's demeanor, we guessed most of those in attendance were against the bill. A veterinarian from our area testified for the bill, stating how dogs' legs are deformed from being confined in a puppy mill and their health compromised, which was true of our dear Bonnie.

Then, a lady who had sled dogs complained that she needed to breed to replace a sled dog when one got old.

I leaned over to David and said, "What a bunch of hooey. The bill defines a breeder as someone with more than five females. How many dogs is she going to have to replace in one year? She doesn't need five females who can breed."

It was apparent people were at this meeting to protect their pocketbooks. We did not get a chance to say anything that day, but what we heard against this bill was infuriating and disheartening. We later learned that a task force was convened to determine the definition of a breeder and what government agency would have oversight. When you are afraid to take action, convene a committee.

I kept checking on the status and finally got in touch with the woman in charge of the task force. She sounded apologetic, explaining what they had accomplished with hesitancy. She then directed me to the entire bill on the state website.

Discouraged after reading the guidelines, I decided to put together my thoughts on what could be done, calling for a $2,000 license fee a year for breeders and a fee for every dog bred. Also, a higher license fee for non-spayed and non-neutered dogs.

Back then and still today, the fee for licensing a spayed or neutered dog is $10-12 in most cities, and for non-spayed/neutered dogs, it is $12-15, a difference of a few dollars. Many of the dogs in shelters are the result of dog companions not spaying Fido and Sadie, so the fee needed to encourage them to spay and neuter.

Besides increasing fees, it is important to restrict how often a female dog could be bred—only once every two years was my recommendation. That way fewer puppies would be born, and female dogs would not be abused.

You might be saying that would increase the price of a puppy so breeders can keep their profits high. So, why should that be a guiding force? Why would anyone want to protect those who breed countless dogs repeatedly or contribute to their pocketbooks?

I then sent my proposal to every representative in both the House and Senate in the state. Only one representative got in touch with me and was anxious to do something about the puppy mills and irresponsible breeding.

About a week after she proposed the bill, she sent me an e-mail. She had pulled the bill. It was clear there was an outcry against the bill that she was not prepared to face. She, too, appeared shaken and upset by the calls and e-mails she had received from constituents and breeders, plus comments from her colleagues.

I ask myself over and over again when will people get angry enough to fight for the rights of dogs? Why is it taking so long for us to do something to stop our best friends from suffering?

Maybe we need a campaign of national awareness—awareness about how dogs are bred and the joy and happiness of rescuing. I can't say this enough, "You may think that you are rescuing a dog, but that dog is rescuing you. You just don't know it yet."

Chapter 9
A Return and An Arrival

Three riveting pairs of bright eyes
Fixed on the movements of my hand
Cupboard love or devotion?
Maybe both; doesn't matter.

A puppy-mill owner had robbed Bonnie of her puppyhood and her health. These things we could not give her back, but we were determined to making sure she felt safe and loved.

A few weeks after being spayed, Bonnie was ready for adoption. We struggled to let her go. We were mindful that she was so needy and so loving, so it would be best for her to be the only dog. Then an adoption counselor called. A couple was interested in Bonnie, particularly the husband.

When I spoke with the adopter, he told me he wanted a dog that would "hang with him." His former dog was independent and was not interested in spending time by his side. I realize now that was a clue.

He desired a dog who would be by his side 24/7. I explained several times that Bonnie was indeed clingy and asked, "Do you really want a clingy dog?" He assured me he did. It definitely seemed like the perfect match.

When he and his wife arrived the following Saturday, I gave them both a treat to give to Bonnie.

When Bonnie came into the living room, the man was busy talking about something. Although he did not greet her with much enthusiasm, he scratched behind her ears.

That was a second clue—resisting a dog like Bonnie, especially knowing her history, should have been difficult, if you are a dog lover. Bonnie was a gorgeous dog. Yes, she had a sweet face, with long, lush ears and grab-your-heart brown eyes, and she was such a gentle soul. And Bonnie, like Zoey, was hesitant and hung back until she was called.

The Mrs. called Bonnie to her and gave her the treat. Bonnie sat on the floor next to her while her husband talked and talked. She petted Bonnie while we chatted and the Mr. talked with David. I liked the calm demeanor of the Mrs. and how she responded to Bonnie.

Finally, the Mr. said, "She doesn't seem to like me."

"I don't think we have any way of knowing that yet. You still have that treat in your hand, and you haven't called her to you or given her much attention."

He took the hint. He called Bonnie over and gave her the treat. It was then that he petted her and rubbed under her ears.

Finally, I asked him what he thought about Bonnie. He smiled and said she was pretty and a sweet dog. He thought they would get along fine together.

Every day she had broken my heart. Now she was a happy dog, and I wanted her to go to a home where she would get loads of pets and hugs, a home where she would be treasured. As they drove away, I couldn't help but wonder. I knew the Mrs. would treasure her. I just wasn't sure of him.

Most likely, the Mrs. would also be the caretaker, so that gave me some consolation. I knew he would not harm Bonnie, but I was not convinced he could treasure any dog. Knowing something of the human condition, he appeared to me incapable, but I had no proof.

The next time we left the house to pick up a foster dog, I said to David, "Samson is probably nudging Delilah right now and saying, 'What are they going to bring home for us this time?'"

Then we laughed, and I added, "I'm so proud of them. They're such great dogs."

I believed that we had been successful with the fosters—the training, their respecting the bowl and each other's treats, calmness, and learning how to live in a home—because Samson and Delilah helped lead the way.

The following weekend we got a call to take in two more fosters. It was December, and they had been found in a barn in the cold northern part of our state and were being spayed. Their names—given to them by someone in our organization—were Belle and Chanté. We agreed to take them, of course.

That Saturday, we were excited about picking up these two little girls who would soon enjoy the comfort and warmth of a home.

The transport car was already there when we pulled up in the parking lot at the meeting place. On one end of the lead was one of our devoted volunteers and on the other end a small dog with a wide-track stance.

As we approached, the volunteer yelled out, "This one's a keeper."

I looked down at a spotted dog that was a beagle and something else. "It looks that way. She looks like she's smiling. Where's the other one?"

"What other one?"

"When Sam (he was the intake director) called, he asked us to take two fosters. I just wonder where she is?"

"This is the only one I was asked to bring. This is Belle."

"Then, it's Chanté that is missing."

David put her on my lap, and on the way home, we cooed and petted her. She had a barrel chest and short paws and was very huggable—like all the rest. Her ears were long and floppy, and her overall demeanor and ticking were beagle-like. She had the most gorgeous thick coat.

There was something about this dog that took hold of both of us. I could feel it. We talked about her name, neither of us caring much for Belle. It wasn't enough of a name for her.

I had read that a dog's name should be at least two syllables, so when you said it, you could draw it out—Sam....son.... De....li...lah. That way, it was easier for the dog to learn.

So, we played around with her name, and on the way home, we changed her name from Belle to LittleBit. I always wanted to name a dog LittleBit and did so in a fictional tale I wrote to teach personality types. It seemed to be the perfect name for her, given her size.

After agreeing on LittleBit, which took all of three seconds, I said to David, "We can't change her name. When she gets adopted, they will want her to know the name Belle. That will be the name on the website."

"Who says we're going to give her up."

I chuckled. "Well, I don't know. We'll have to see what Samson and Delilah say about it. Not being a pure beagle may make it difficult to get her adopted. We always said that if a dog can't get adopted," and then we said in unison, "We would adopt the dog."

Then David said in a low voice, "Samson and Delilah are getting older…."

Neither of us could say the words. We knew that the day would come when we would lose our original two—a name we had given them—and the pain would be devastating.

David wanted to have other dogs in the house WHEN, although for me no other dog could replace Samson or Delilah or make the heartbreak easier. Also, I always wanted a pack of four, although I never thought it would happen. LittleBit would get us closer to that desire.

Immediately, Samson came running to LittleBit, and they raced around the driveway. LittleBit ran at hyper-speed, and although her legs were short, Samson had difficulty keeping up with her. Within minutes she and Samson had become playmates.

Delilah, as she did with all our fosters, greeted her with a wagging tail and even bounced around, trying to engage her in play.

That evening we went upstairs to the bedroom. All three rushing up the steps. LittleBit knew where she wanted to be. She immediately cuddled beside Samson on a bed, the two of them spooning. We were thrilled.

Over the last several months, with Bonnie unable to engage him in play and Delilah too demure to roughhouse for long periods, he had become a couch potato, even though he was only seven.

The following day I called to find out what happened to Chanté.

Sam chuckled. "We adopted her on the spot. My wife fell in love."

"Well, we might be keeping the one you sent us."

In the bag that came with LittleBit was ointment for her eyes. We took her to our vet for a follow-up visit. Her eyes were always red and weeping.

Our vet put some yellow liquid in her eyes. "That yellow liquid should be coming out of her nose, and it isn't. Her tear ducts are permanently blocked." He then dropped his head and said in a mellow voice, "She will cry all her life."

"Is there anything that can be done?" I asked.

"Stop using that ointment. It's not helping and may be causing LittleBit's eyes more problems. She could have an operation to unblock the ducts, but I'm not sure it's the best idea. She's not in pain, but she will always have drainage from her eyes."

We hugged her to us, and the vet couldn't help but smile. She was so darn cute.

Then the day we had dreaded happened. The phone rang, and it was an adoption counselor asking if we would take Bonnie back.

"Of course, we'll take sweet Bonnie back, but what happened?"

"The man said she was too clingy."

"That's what he said he wanted, and now he doesn't?"

"I don't know, Elizabeth."

I decided to find out more, so I probed. Finally, the adoption counselor shared that this was the second dog the adopter had returned. He had adopted another dog a few weeks before and returned that dog because she was not clingy enough.

"So, why did we try with him again, and why didn't I know that? If I did, I would have never let him meet her."

"I guess you should have known."

"What about the wife? Did she agree with this decision?"

"I spoke with the wife because the husband was probably too embarrassed to speak with me. It was not her idea to return Bonnie. She liked her. I don't think she agreed, but the dog was for him."

I was upset and trying to make sense of it, so I blurted out, "Maybe Bonnie liked the wife too much. When the couple was here, Bonnie seemed to like her best.

"He even expressed concern that she did not like him. If when they got home, she followed the wife around instead of him…. Well.... How sad. We're not going to give him a third try, are we?"

"No, we're not."

"Hallelujah!"

Chapter 10
Welcoming Bonnie Back

Three fluffy beds were strewn around
All three pooches on a single one
Squirming and jostling for comfort
Now settled down together. Lovely!

We all welcomed Bonnie back. Giving Bonnie up had been just one too many losses, and now having her returned was crushing.

LittleBit was such a lovely dog, carefree and joyful, as besotted with Samson as we were with her. What added to our joy was that she and Delilah were often cuddling together. As independent as Delilah was, we always wanted another dog that loved them both.

The following week, two weeks after LittleBit's arrival, I confirmed her adoption by saying to David, "Let's give LittleBit to each other as a Christmas present."

Christmas was just a week away. We had finally failed as a foster family. David was not that fond of the term, failed foster. We just fell in forever love, and that was not a failure.

The five of us, plus Bonnie, had settled into a happy family, enjoying the antics of LittleBit and Samson and the sweetness of Bonnie and Delilah.

However, LittleBit in time wasn't so sure about Bonnie. Bonnie was getting the attention she wanted. I started to call her, "Me three." Samson still owned the name, "Me two."

Our answer about Bonnie's forever home came a few weeks later. A young woman wanted to adopt her. When an adoption has failed, it is scary to let that dog go a second time. We also had to remember we had to love her enough to let her go if it were best for her.

The adoption counselor told me that this potential adopter was a single woman. She wanted a "clingy" dog. Where have I heard that before?

I learned from our conversation that she and her boyfriend had moved in together and purchased a beagle. About a year later, she came home one day to find that he was gone and had taken the dog. She was still heartbroken and wanted to adopt a dog that needed her.

After speaking with the young woman, I was impressed with her willingness to give Bonnie a wonderful life. Maybe they would heal each other.

When the day came to deliver Bonnie to her forever home, it was with a hopeful heart and a tearful goodbye that we handed Bonnie over to a transporter.

We both hugged her, and I kissed her head and looked into those soulful eyes.

I said to David as we drove away, "I hope she will be happy. She has suffered enough for three lifetimes."

Within days I got an e-mail from Bonnie's adopter saying she had fallen in love, and all was great. Yes, it did turn out to be Bonnie's forever home. She loved her to bits.

We were again a family of five. For how long was always an unknown.

Chapter 11
Stubborn and Cute Wrapped in One

I can't think of anything that brings me closer to tears than when my old dog—completely exhausted after a hard day in the field—limps away from her nice spot in front of the fire and comes over to where I'm sitting and puts her head in my lap, a paw over my knee, and closes her eyes and goes back to sleep.

Gene Hill

A few months before LittleBit arrived, we had remodeled a bathroom. We put the tub where the dogs slept in the new bathroom, so a daybed was added to our bedroom for the dogs. We also decided to get a queen-size bed because often, we ended up with all three dogs in our bed anyway. First, Samson would jump in, and LittleBit wanted to join him.

LittleBit—well, her legs were so short—she couldn't jump on any of our beds. She threw her body against the side of the bed, her stubby paws holding onto the edge. Then she looked around at us as if saying, "Can anyone give me a lift," which we were more than happy to do.

Delilah stayed on her bed—always a good dog until she was called. Then she would jump up, delighted for the opportunity to be cuddled.

With LittleBit, it soon becomes apparent that we had finally gotten a stubborn one in a delightful way, and this intrigued me. Beagles get a rap for being stubborn, but we hadn't found that to be so with the many beagles we had fostered and even our "original two." All were sweet, gentle souls, even Samson, in spite of his high energy. Yet, along came a mixed beagle who, we had decided, had Jack Russell in her DNA, and the stubborn gene surfaced.

When she didn't want to walk anymore, LittleBit planted her four paws as though they were in concrete. We called and called, and she would sit on the driveway looking at us as though she were a cat. Frequently, we were convinced she was saying to us: "You want me to come to you? Me? I don't come on command."

Of course, her hangdog look and her soft eyes melted our hearts and made us laugh. Still, at times it could be irritating, especially when the other dogs were in a hurry to get moving.

LittleBit was also the first dog, including Samson and Delilah and all the fosters, who would not accept the leader collar, which I believed contributed to her stubbornness. We would put it on, and immediately she would sit down and not move. She loved to walk, but not with the leader collar. She did have a more prominent snout, and we discovered that the strap slipped down and hit the edges of her mouth, which might have bothered her.

Sometimes we gave in to her and walked her using a harness, but other times we insisted on the leader collar. Then, she would move grudgingly, poking along without any enthusiasm and keeping her head low, grumbling and groaning.

It was disheartening to watch a joyful dog who had such high energy not enjoying the adventures outside the gate. When we removed the leader collar, she was a different dog, strutting along as though she were in charge. We talked about not using it, but then one of us would say, "Are we in charge, or is she?" so we persevered.

LittleBit had attitude, and we loved that about her. She sashayed when she walked, visited with everyone we passed, if they were so inclined, and made her presence known everywhere she went. Often, she made a grunting sound when she walked up to strangers. Then I heard, "Oh, she's talking to me." Indeed, she was a talker and such a sweet one.

One day I spied the perfect Christmas stocking for LittleBit. It was bright red in the shape of a huge dog bone with the writing, "Santa, it's all about me." Indeed, that could be said about our sweet girl.

We noticed almost immediately that LittleBit did not sleep all through the night. Any slight movement, she was up, while Samson and Delilah, who knew the routine and felt safe and content, were snuggled down, not moving a muscle. The reason finally occurred to me.

"I bet she's still living in the barn. Imagine every night having to watch out for rats and other animals. Imagine!"

"Well, soon, she'll feel safe and sleep through the night."

She often snorted or snored. I started calling her our "resident pig."

We laughed, delighting in her antics. The snorting did not bother us and, in fact, was quite endearing. Many nights our two little girls snored away, with never a sound from Samson.

Our days were filled with hugs and pets and walks and laughter. David still called the dogs "time wasters," but I always replied, "Such a lovely way to waste time."

We both spent as much time as we could and often more than we had petting and talking with them, taking them to the beach or into town for a walk, and cuddling them. Loving our dogs made every day special.

Chapter 12
The Sweetness of Bella

I think dogs are the most amazing creatures; they give unconditional love. For me, they are the role model for being alive.

Gilda Radner

After we adopted LittleBit, I started singing to the dogs, "We are family. I've got all my beagles with me," again and again. (I just love The Birdcage.) They danced around me with delight and raced around the room. The sound of a happy voice seemed to be music to their ears. I say that because I cannot carry a tune.

An elderly lady whose husband had passed away surrendered seven dogs to the rescue group, including Belle (yes, another one), an eight-year-old dog that we agreed to foster. Over the years, the lady's husband had accumulated ten beagles. After his passing, she had decided to keep three of the younger dogs and surrendered the remaining older ones.

In some way, I could understand why she had made that decision. The younger dogs would be with her longer, maybe, and her vet bills would be less. They had really been his dogs, so possibly she had not become attached to any of them, and so on.

It was now up to the rescue group to find homes for seven older dogs, which often is a challenge.

As volunteers, we were continually getting updates from the rescue group about the dogs adopted with the details. In time I noticed that many of our foster homes would adopt their older fosters and those with health problems or disabilities. This happened most often when a particular family had fostered a dog for many months and even a year or more.

After several years with the rescue group, I took on the responsibility of adoption counselor. When I spoke with adopters, over and over again, I heard, "We want a female, one to three years old."

Before Belle arrived, I had renamed her Bella, which suited her. When I first saw her, I was struck by her calmness. She had become gray, and her tough-life brown color was soft and lovely. There seemed to be pain behind her light brown eyes. She came to me, her ears back against her head, often a sign of fear.

I stopped what I was doing, too many times to count each day, and petted her and scratched behind her ears and under her chin. She touched my heart, and it became challenging to tear myself away from her and get on with whatever I wanted to do.

All three of the pack welcomed her, and LittleBit, who had shown signs of jealousy toward Bonnie, did not seem to be affected by the presence of this new dog in the house. Perhaps that was because LittleBit herself was now more settled and secure, and Bella was not interested in playing with Samson.

About two weeks after Bella's arrival, a past adopter wanted to adopt her. There was no home visit because she had been approved to adopt in the past. My only role was to discuss how we would get Bella to her.

When I spoke with Bella's soon-to-be human companion, I learned that one of her two male dogs had passed away. She also mentioned that her bed was relatively high and believed Bella would have difficulty jumping on the bed to sleep with her.

I told her that we had steps that David had made for our LittleBit. I had abandoned them because I kept tripping over them in the night, and besides, LittleBit preferred a lift. We would be happy to bring the steps with us. She lived about twenty miles away, and because of her traveling problems, we agreed to deliver Bella to her home.

When we arrived at the door, Bella was greeted with hugs and pets from the adopter, as Buster, her male dog, came running toward us, causing me to lose my footing. Immediately, Buster started rousting Bella as the adopter cooed over how special Bella was. Within seconds, Bella jumped on the couch to avoid being mauled, sitting there like a princess—demure and calm.

We were shown around the house, the backyard, and the fenced-in area. We heard about the dog she had lost and looked at the pictures on the wall. The entire time I had my eyes on Buster, watching his attempts to engage Bella in rough play. Only one thought came to mind—he was a bully and quite aggressive—not a playboy like Samson. It was not his fault. He had never been corrected and trained.

The longer we stayed, the more concerns I had about leaving Bella in this home. Finally, I had to say to the adopter, "I'm not sure I want to leave Bella here. Your male dog is too aggressive. You don't seem to have any control over what he does. He does whatever he wants."

David nodded in agreement and added, "He's too rough."

"Oh, please. I just love Bella already. She'll be fine."

"But what about Buster here? How will she be with him? Are you going to make sure she's not harassed by him day-in and day-out?"

After a few minutes of discussion, I turned to David. "What do you think?"

"I don't think we should leave her."

Again, the adopter insisted. "She'll be fine. He's a good dog. I've adopted dogs before, and they have all been fine."

I was not convinced that was true. Buster's behavior was an indication that she had not put in the time and effort to train him to curb his behavior and wasn't exercising him enough.

"Look, I know you like her, and I'm sure you will treat her fine. It's Buster."

"I'll make sure she's OK. Please leave her."

What could I do? She was an approved adopter, and at that time, the foster parents were not able to nix an adoption. If I did not leave Bella, she could be missing out on a good home, but then there were other good homes.

"OK, I will leave her with you, but you have to promise to return her if there is any problem. Promise!"

I spoke with the adopter a few days later, and she told me that everything was great. Bella had mastered the steps we had left in the bedroom for her, and she was enjoying having two dogs cuddled next to her at night. Maybe we were wrong? Maybe? I knew I would ask myself whether this was the best decision for Bella for many weeks.

Chapter 13
Indestructible Delilah

Wishing and hoping forever together
Not one for wishing and hoping
Wishing and hoping for eternity
Their hearts and mine as one

Over the years, fatty tumors had popped up on Delilah's body. We had kept a close eye and hand on Delilah to check them. The first one was on her rump area. The next one was under her arm. Then more appeared on her neck. Another one popped up under the other arm. Again and again, our vet told us that these lumps were most likely fat deposits and were not tumors.

I researched and learned that if they did not grow legs and attach themselves and felt free-floating, they were not cancerous. Delilah also had warts in several places—a large one on her neck. Here and there, another one would appear, just like the fatty lumps. We were told to watch them for changes but were advised not to have them removed.

A few weeks after Bella's adoption, I found a growth on Samson's leg. It felt attached to the tissues beneath, and that worried us. Samson had never had any growths. We rushed him to our vet, and he expressed concern and removed the growth the following day.

For the next few days, we waited impatiently for the report from the lab. It was indeed a malignant tumor, but our vet was convinced he had removed all of it. His only caution was to check him to ensure others did not appear, especially on that leg or chest.

Shortly after this scare with Samson, we found some blood oozing from Delilah's nose. I panicked because I had lost my dog Boomer to sinus cancer years before. That had started with a nose bleed. Again, we rushed to the vet.

The vet believed it could be cancer in her sinuses or caused by her teeth. The vet after x-rays decided it was her teeth, and she would have to have several removed.

We scheduled an appointment, and on the day of the surgery, the vet doing the operation took an x-ray and found that her heart appeared to be enlarged. The vet would not perform the operation unless we took her for a sonogram and got clearance concerning her heart condition.

We met with the specialist the following week. Although Delilah did have a heart problem, it was considered minor. She did not need any medication and was cleared for the operation. Of course, when we took her in, I told the vet tech, "Tell the doctor, just the minimal anesthesia."

A few hours later, we got the long-awaited call from the vet. "Delilah is awake and is fine."

After the call, I hugged Samson and LittleBit to me and then searched for David to tell him the good news.

One of the things Samson and Delilah reminded me of is that dogs pay attention to their human companions.

How we treat one dog affects the other, just like with children.

Remember the second Bella, the sweet girl we didn't want to leave with the adopter because we feared how Bella would fare with her other dog Buster?

The adopter got in touch with me a few months later, reporting that Bella was exhibiting some troublesome behavior. A lot of inappropriate dog behavior is often at the other end of the lead, and I wasn't going to deny my instinct this time. There was no doubt the adopter and her inability to deal with Buster was the problem. There was no such behavior when she was with us, and we had three other dogs.

There was much written on the subject, including why this particular behavior surfaces. Knowing why was more or at least as important as what to do. One leading cause cited was something or someone was upsetting Bella and making her nervous.

I wrote the adopter a supportive note, telling her this could be corrected and making some suggestions. I also pointed out that since nervousness was the leading cause, she needed to monitor the dynamics between Bella and Buster more closely.

I also sent along several pages of information and suggestions with some websites to check out. Of course, one of the things I stressed was that she needed to take action. She needed to be present and train Buster. Bella could not take that action.

I followed up about a week later with more information, asking how Bella was doing. I did not hear anything. Over a month later, I received another e-mail saying, "I'm at the end of my rope. Maybe I should return Bella."

She said again she was not sure what to do. I knew my suggestions would take time and energy, and she wasn't willing to take the time. I also knew that dog owners often do not want to correct their dogs for fear the dogs would not like them. Such a silly notion that dogs surely don't understand. They are looking for a leader, seeking direction. If she wasn't willing to change the dynamics in her house, then Buster's behavior would continue, and Bella would continue to suffer.

I agreed that she should return Bella, and she responded by scolding me and telling me that no way would Bella be removed from her care. Surprise!

Although she had suggested it, I'm at fault. I was supportive and wanted her to feel better about this decision, and, of course, I wanted Bella out of that house.

I guess she wanted me to tell her, "Oh no. You should keep her. This can be worked out."

In reality, she wanted me to be sympathetic. I could not be. She had promised me she would protect Bella, but doing so would take time, energy, and a willingness to deal with Buster's behavior. In reality, she wanted a quick fix, and from what I could tell, little involvement. I felt inconsolable regret that I had left Bella in that home.

She was irresponsible. Irresponsible dog owners don't train their dogs to live in a home, don't get up in the morning and take the dog outside, don't manage the pack dynamic, such as "respect the bowl," allow one dog to bully another, and so on.

The world we have put dogs in doesn't allow for their independence. Just as a child wants a parent to be protective and monitor the family dynamics, dogs are no different. That means not allowing one child or dog to harm another or hold the entire family hostage.

In the end, Bella was to stay with the adopter, and I was no longer involved. I often say people are messy, and this was one of those messy times.

Some might consider that I/we have a flaw in surrendering our fosters to a new home—just a little too fussy. I would say discriminating. But my mantra is, "Every dog should have a home. Not every human should have a dog."

As a foster parent, it is difficult to surrender a dog to an adopter. But what makes it most difficult is surrendering a dog you have cared for, often for weeks and sometimes for many months, into the wrong home.

The rescue group had put together a system with checks and balances that assured due diligence was done, but people are the variable. No matter how thorough the initial interview, the application, the reference check, and the home visit were, only so much can be learned during that process.

We fostered dogs to help them on their journey, and if I made a human unhappy or angry along the way, so be it. The dog should always win every time. Someone had to be their voice.

I would never forgive myself for not taking Bella with us on that day, no matter the consequences. My heart will forever feel sorrow about that adoption.

Chapter 14
Millie and Sallie

One of the greatest gifts we receive from dogs is the tenderness they evoke in us.
Dean Koontz, A Big Little Life

Often, we did not hear about the foster dogs after they left us. We were happy to get a note about Bonnie, the puppy mill, blue-tick beagle. Dear Bonnie was much loved by all.

There they were—another pair of one-year-old female dogs. Now we would have five dogs to pet, feed, walk, hug, and pet.

When I told David the news, he said, "How will we walk five dogs?"

"We have the double leads you made when we had Sissy and Snoopy."

The only information we had about these two girls was that they were "failed hunters." This term is used for dogs that have been bought to hunt but then refuse or fail to do so even after training. We also knew that they were from the same litter.

When I first saw them, I was struck by their visual differences. Sallie was slender and was jumping out of her skin—racing around the parking lot where we picked them up. Her face was thin, and her stature small—only 13 inches.

Millie was stocky but not heavy, standing next to the volunteer. Her big eyes were fixed on Sallie, and she had beautiful markings and deep-rich, russet brown and black—no white. Were these two Thelma and Louise all over again?

Samson was taken within seconds by Sallie's energy, so they immediately became playmates. Samson now had to share his playtime with LittleBit and Sallie.

We soon realized we did not have the full scoop on these two little girls, especially Millie.

"How could someone even think of making a hunter out of Millie?" I said to David. "She's afraid of every sound." I dropped a spoon on the kitchen floor to demonstrate. Millie skedaddled under the table, running as fast as she could.

David nodded. "It's the same as Louise, that dog that would never come in the house."

"Well, no, not quite. Louise was afraid of people. Millie wants to be loved and will come at the sound of my voice. She's just afraid of loud sounds. My gosh, what happened when a gun was fired? She must have panicked. But why was Sallie given up? She's not afraid of anything."

David called Millie towards him and petted her. "She's a gentle dog."

"She's a sweetheart. Look at those eyes. Melts your heart."

Within an hour, Sallie settled in, playing with Samson and dragging stuffed toys out of the house. By mid-day, there were at least six toys strewn around my flower garden. I laughed when I looked outside and saw a stuffed teddy bear, a chipmunk, a bunny, a skunk, two stuffed dogs, and several balls—adding many unintended colors and interest to my garden.

As with our other dogs, we decided to allow these two girls to sleep in our bedroom rather than leave them alone in the kitchen. I was tempted because Sallie was so rambunctious, and I wasn't sure she would settle down. I took them up to the bedroom for Millie's sake. I wanted her to feel secure.

We learned almost immediately that Sallie had a short attention span—stayed a few seconds and then raced away to play. I said to David, "I think she's a dog's dog, not a people dog."

David nodded, knowing what I meant. Although I found it rare with beagles, some dogs seem more interested in dogs than people. Sallie was definitely one of them. Although she and Samson played non-stop at times, Samson wanted pets and hugs, too, any attention he could get from us. He would leave his food for a kind word or pet. Most people would think that's very rare for a beagle, but that was our Samson boy.

Millie settled in too, but it was on one of the dog beds. She was content to be snuggled down by herself or with Delilah, who welcomed her. Often, Samson and Sallie would romp and play together, while LittleBit stayed on the sidelines. Sallie had replaced LittleBit as Samson's playmate. That caused me sadness and concern because Sallie's presence had changed the dynamics of our beagle pack.

With Sallie, there was no way for LittleBit to join in. As a result, I often sequestered Samson and LittleBit into an area where they could romp and play together without Sallie's interference. I felt it was my responsibility to manage the play dynamics. Samson or LittleBit could not.

Remember, I said that not all fosters should become members of your pack. Sallie was definitely one of those. I could not allow anything to spoil LittleBit's comfort and happiness. She had loved Samson from the beginning, and I would never want anything to harm that relationship by adopting Sallie.

Until Sallie was adopted, Samson and LittleBit could not return to being a twosome. Also, I knew it would be challenging to get Millie adopted, and we had to decide whether the two girls should stay together.

Once again, we questioned where we would find someone who would be patient enough with Millie. Would she ever be desensitized to sounds and how to do that? Dogs do not come with instruction manuals.

Several times a day, I would make a loud sound on purpose, sometimes the same sound repeatedly. My hope was that eventually, the clattering would become commonplace and no longer frightening to her.

I also tried to redirect Millie's attention to something pleasant, or I called her to me and calmed her down. These tactics were met with limited success. After about a week, I realized that she could spend the rest of her life being skittish.

One day after a session with Millie, I said to David, "I think it would be best if Millie went to a quiet home with a single person or an elderly couple who has a calmer life than in a family with young children. Also, if there are other dogs in the home, they need to be older or low-keyed."

"She doesn't seem to be getting any better, does she?"

"Not really with the sounds, but she is comfortable with our dogs and us. No fears there. That makes her adoptable."

We had agreed to foster Millie and Sallie because we thought it would be kinder to keep them together.

Speaking with one of the volunteers, she confirmed our thinking that maybe they should be adopted separately. She explained that often one sibling becomes dominant and the other submissive. In my words, "One of them never gets her wings" until they get away from the other, if indeed they can withstand the separation.

When I shared this thought with David, we reflected on our time with Thelma and Louise, Like Louise, Millie was in the background, both dominated by their siblings.

Also, like Thelma, David and I knew that Sallie would get adopted quickly. She was the right age, female, a good-looking beagle, and fun and full of life.

Fortunately, it was summer, and all the dogs loved the outdoors. About three weeks after their arrival, there were adopters for Sallie who had young children and a young male dog who needed a playmate. Perfect for Sallie, so off she went.

Immediately after Sallie was adopted, Millie began to emerge from her shell. She was still nervous at sudden sounds, but she romped and played with Samson and LittleBit and did not shy away from a new experience. It was as though a frightening force has been lifted from her and that frightening force, we believed, was Sallie. Nothing else had changed.

About two weeks later, the family who adopted Sallie wanted to adopt Millie too. This was not the home for Millie. Two hyperactive dogs and children. When I expressed my concerns about this adoption, I was told that the decision had been made.

So far, you may realize that dog rescue groups are much-needed and worthwhile organizations, so I want to stop in the middle of this story to clarify something about rescue groups. First, rescue groups are volunteer organizations, so all the money raised and donations are spent on the dogs. The foster families incur all the expenses while the foster dogs are in their homes. The volunteers who transport a dog pay for the gas and give up a morning or afternoon.

Volunteers raise money, transport, foster, conduct home visits, speak with adopters, and do whatever is necessary to help hundreds of dogs each year. No salaries are paid. David and I were just two of over a hundred people vested in helping these dogs.

Like most rescue organizations, the volunteers are made up of dog lovers with different experiences with dogs, different philosophies about training and behavior, and so on. Like most rescue groups, we had some of the most devoted, loving volunteers who would do anything for the dogs.

But like any other organization, once in a while, people have different opinions and different ways of looking at the same situation. This was one of those times.

While speaking with the adopter, I became more agitated about turning sweet Millie over to this home.

I said to David, "I don't want to send Millie to that house. Sallie is resilient, and I'm sure she's fine. Millie needs patience and quiet, and not two dogs racing around...."

David looked puzzled. "What is bothering you about this adopter?"

"I don't think the home is right for Millie. They have a high-energy male dog and wanted Sallie as a playmate. Where does Millie fit into the pack? They don't need her too."

David shook his head. "Do you think she would return Sallie if they don't get Millie?"

"It doesn't matter. Millie is happier now without Sallie. These last two weeks—it's like she's a different dog."

Millie reminded me of Bonnie. So gentle, loving, and in need of a kind and gentle hand. That weekend, we were sad that we had to send Millie on her way. Deep down, I believed and somewhat hoped we would see her again.

Unlike Bella's adopter, who would not give her up, I wish this one would be more compassionate if it were not a good match.

Chapter 15
For the Love of Millie

"*My fashion philosophy is if you're not covered in dog hair, your life is empty.*"

Elayne Boosler

Remember, I said we had a revolving door in our house. The following week our next foster arrived. Lacey was found on the streets, and it was December. The vet's record puts her age around three years old, although I believed her to be older.

When we first saw Lacey, I was struck by her resemblance to Samson. She looked like a smaller version of him. Her eyes were soulful, and she had a gentle demeanor. When we arrived home, Samson immediately raced to greet Lacey, and once again, he had a rollicking playmate.

One of Samson's nicknames was "toy boy" because he loved to play with toys, but I said to David, "I think we should change Samson's name to playboy. How many female dogs has he taken as his own?"

David chuckled, "Well, they all seem to like him."

I noticed that Lacey had stitches. When I reviewed the vet records, I discovered that the vet had tried to spay her but found she was already spayed. Oh my, how could that mistake have been made? Then I knew that someone must have cared for her, someone must have wanted her at one time, so why was she now in our home?

We were a family of six until the phone rang about ten days later. It was an adoption counselor asking us if we would be willing to foster Millie again.

"Why, what happened? How is she?"

"The adopters want her out of the house today."

"Why, what did she do?"

"I'm not sure, Elizabeth. I'm a new adoption counselor. This was my first adoption. I told the woman that Millie was nervous and afraid of sounds. She told me that she had dealt with such dogs before. Her behavior would not be a problem. I believed her, but I guess she lied or exaggerated the truth of the matter."

I was confused but responded, "She won't be the first or the last. But why do we have to get Mille out tonight? The adopters had her for almost two weeks."

"No, no. The adopters had Millie for only one night. I can't imagine she did many things wrong. She's just too skittish."

"What do you mean they had her for one night? What happened with the couple who adopted Millie two weeks ago?"

"They returned her, so we had another adopter waiting for a dog. They picked her up yesterday. They had her one night. Now they want her out of the house immediately. Not tomorrow, but tonight."

"But I don't understand why she was tossed out of the first home?"

"Apparently, they came home one day, and she was on top of the buffet. They said she was growling, and I'm not sure what else?"

"Millie would never do such a thing unless provoked and afraid, nor could she jump on top of a buffet. Have you seen her? She's anything but agile."

"That's what the woman said."

"Well, she exaggerated the truth or Millie was so traumatized by something in that home, she maneuvered herself there to get away from either the kids or the two other dogs."

As I was saying that, I knew it did not matter. Millie had to get out of the home she was in now. Although my upset had not subsided, I got myself together long enough to say, "Of course, we will take her back, but only on one condition. I have to be involved in the next adoption. I will not let her go if I have reservations about the adopter."

There was silence on the other end of the phone. I continued, "I was concerned about Millie's first adopter and disagreed with the decision. I told the other adoption counselor that we would welcome Millie back but only if I had a voice in the next adoption."

"I guess we should have spoken to you, but the woman was happy about getting her...." She paused, "Elizabeth, I will involve you in the adoption, but please could you get Millie today? The husband is willing to bring her near your home."

She told me the town's name, about forty minutes away, and the exit from the highway.

"What time will he be there?"

"4 o'clock."

"We'll be there."

Within a half-hour, we were on the road. I admitted to David that I was looking forward to seeing Millie again. Yet, I was concerned about how she might have changed due to what had happened to her during the last two weeks.

When the car arrived, we saw a middle-aged man with Millie on the lead. I raced to her and hugged her, and David picked her up in his arms. I took the bag he handed me. No words were spoken by any of us.

David put Millie on my lap, and when he got in the car, he said, "I wanted to clobber him…."

"I don't think he had a say. I think it was the wife! That's why she didn't come with him. She couldn't face us after bragging that she knew how to handle nervous dogs."

I went through the bag that came with Millie and found two different bottles of tranquilizers. Millie's name was on the bottle and the name of the first adopters. What had Millie gone through? Again, we would never know.

When we arrived home, Samson, Delilah, LittleBit, and Lacey greeted Millie. She went to a bed, and it was as though she had never left us. Over the next several days that turned into weeks, Millie was content. She would play outside with the other dogs. Then come in and settle on her favorite bed, often with Delilah, or a comfy chair alone.

Then, you guessed it. The phone rang. There were adopters for Millie. I spoke at length to both. Their last dog was partly beagle and had passed away a few months before. They were looking for a low-keyed dog.

The wife had an illness that limited her energy level, and she spent her days relaxing or in bed. They had no children, and the husband was out all day at work. It appeared to be the perfect quiet home for Millie. She would have this couple's undivided attention, especially her mistress during the day. The noise level would be minimal.

Yet, with all the positives, I was having difficulty getting excited about this adoption. It's difficult to surrender a dog to an adopter, but more so when it has been returned, and in this case twice. Also, I wondered if the wife had grieved long enough over her last dog. Most of our conversation was her telling me about the dog that passed away.

I was reassured during our two discussions that they would be responsible, loving dog owners. If I had not believed that, I would never have agreed to drive about one hundred miles south that weekend. I wasn't going to turn Millie over to a transporter. I wanted to meet her adopters.

As they greeted Millie, they fussed over her soft ears and sweet face. The two of them took turns petting and talking to her and asking us questions. David took a walk with the Mr. and Millie. The Mrs. pulled out a picture of their other dog and showed it to me. I listened to her talk about the dog she loved and missed.

What to do? Should I let Millie go? These questions kept spinning in my head as she showed David the same pictures when he returned. It was apparent that they were kind people and would never harm Millie.

I also wanted her to have a forever home—sooner rather than later. Every day I had become more attached to her. We knew she could never be our forever dog. She needed to be the only dog in a home where she would have a quiet life. We could not give that to her. Yet, I wanted her to live an extraordinary life in the best home possible.

It was evident that they wanted to adopt Millie and take her with them on that day. It was then I cornered the husband. "You know what Millie's been through."

He nodded as he bowed his head, and I continued. "She's a sweet dog, but she needs patience. I need you to do something for Millie. You have to make it clear to your wife that if she compares Millie to your other dog, she may not be able to withstand the comparison. That's not fair to Millie. Does that make sense? Can you do that?"

He nodded. "I'll talk to her. It will be fine."

I trusted and believed him. Millie was going to what I knew would be her "forever home."

Chapter 16
Handsome Samson Boy

Three furry doggies collapsed around me.
Nestled in a bundle of warmth
Like links of a chain, tail to nose

We are now a family of six again, but for how long? Over the next week, we were anxious about Millie. Then I got a call from the adopting Mom. Millie had settled in wonderfully. Love was in her voice, and I knew Millie would live out her life cherished and pampered. Her hardships were over. Yeah, Millie!

About two weeks after Millie's adoption, we received a call that someone was interested in Lacey. Remember, we were still fostering her.

She played with Samson and LittleBit. More importantly, she was a friend to our sweet Delilah, greeting her with a wagging tail and snuggling with her on a bed.

Many of our previous fosters had not engaged Delilah in these many ways. Now, we had Lacey wanting to play, and at times Delilah would take her up on that offer. We always wanted a playmate for her that was her size and not too rough.

So, we started talking about adopting her, making her our #4. David had fallen head over heels in love with this darling dog, snuggling with him on his chair every night. He forgot the rule of protecting his heart, and he was the one at the beginning who was worried about me falling in forever love.

My hesitancy was twofold. Lacey was a younger dog, and she was adoptable, which violated our adoption rules. But shouldn't love triumph, just this once, after all the dogs we had let go?

Having an adopter waiting in the wings was forcing us to make a decision, so I blurted out to the adoption counselor, "We're thinking of adopting Lacey into our family. Let me talk to David before I talk to these adopters."

David had always been a quick decision-maker. He decided within minutes to adopt Samson and Delilah and then LittleBit. It did not take him more than a few seconds to say that we should adopt Lacey.

The next decision was what to name Lacey. We weren't fond of that name for her. It took a few days, but we finally settled on Sophie.

We also made another decision. We were not going to foster another dog in the near future. We wanted some time for this new family to come together. We wanted to give Sophie and LittleBit more time with us as well.

Samson and Delilah had been with us for almost five years before we started fostering, and we had devoted that time to just them. Now it was an opportunity for these two little girls to get more of what our "original two" had received.

At this time, with four dogs crowding us in bed, we decided to get a king-size bed. Yes, we realized we should have done that instead of getting a queen, but we didn't have a crystal ball.

Samson and Sophie snuggled at the bottom of the bed together. LittleBit tucked in beside David, and Diddle Dee, our sweet Delilah, next to me. Surprisingly, there was just enough room. The dog beds were relegated to the storage closet, and the daybed was empty. We had given in.

It was summer again, and friends, Betty and Walt, were visiting us. We sat on the porch chatting, the dogs scattered around us.

Samson was in his favorite place, sitting beside me and Betty on a loveseat. As Betty was petting him under his ears and down his neck, she felt a lump. I felt it, and my heart literally began to ache. The time we had been dreading. I knew without knowing that this was serious, although I didn't know why. The following day we took our sweet boy to our veterinarian.

"He has lymphoma. It's a form of cancer. It's fatal," said the vet, seeing the tears in my eyes.

"So, what can we do?" I cried.

"Only two choices—chemotherapy or not."

"There's nothing good about those choices. Samson suffers, or he dies."

David looked crushed. "What are his chances?"

I jumped in, "How much will he suffer?"

"Every dog is different. Some stay in remission for a short period, and then we have to do chemo again. Others do not do well."

After more discussion, we decided to do the chemo and see how Samson handled it. We wanted to give him every opportunity to live, but we were still unsure if we had made the right decision.

On the day of Samson's first chemo, we waited for the phone to ring. One of the many things I feared was the anesthesia. Would he wake up each time? Early that afternoon, the phone rang, "I'm calling about Samson," says Dr. H. "All is fine. He woke up, and you can come for him about 4."

"Thank you, thank you," I cried.

Samson was somewhat groggy when we picked him up but thrilled to see us. We were given pills in case he threw up. Fortunately, that did not happen, nor did he seem debilitated. Within three days, the lymph nodes had decreased in size. We were thrilled.

The second round of chemo again went without a hitch, and he did not get ill or seemed harmed. His appetite had not changed, and his lymph nodes continued to shrink.

We took him for the third round, hoping we would all have the same luck. He was listless the day after and stayed on his bed. At nighttime, he threw the covers over his body, as he had taught himself to do many years ago. Then he woke up, found his way out of the covers and panted. Then he shivered. That pattern of panting and shivering was repeated several times. We felt so helpless.

If he appeared to be in distress, we were to call our veterinarian. He had given us his cell number, so we could reach him anytime, even at his home, but we knew he had gone on a trip.

We also did not know what distress looked like and what would be an expected response. We thought this was normal. Yet, I realized we were clueless and definitely not prepared to help Samson through this.

We took Samson for his fourth round of chemo the following week, dreading that day. Our veterinarian was still on vacation, so we spoke with the vet who was taking his appointments.

"Samson has been very ill this past week," I said. "He shivered and then panted repeatedly during most of the night. We think we should skip the chemo this week."

"Well, he seems fine now."

"Yes, but he wasn't fine for three or four days."

He told us that Samson should have the treatment. We should not interrupt it. We did not feel in a position to argue with him, and we believed he would do what was best for Samson and not harm him.

When we picked up Samson that afternoon, not only was he groggy, but he was zapped of all his energy. That night the "foodie" of the family would not eat, no matter what I tried to give him.

We spent the evening cuddling him and holding him to us. We did not know how to help him, so all we could do was stay by his side until morning, never sleeping.

The next day the same thing continued. It was my birthday, and David had planned to take me out to dinner. I did not want to go. I just could not leave Samson alone.

Then I noticed that LittleBit was not in the house or yard. I screamed to David, "LittleBit has gone."

"How did she get out?"

"It doesn't matter how she got out. She's gone!"

David got the keys to the car and was out the gate in minutes, driving around the neighborhood. I could not walk up and down the streets because I wanted to stay with Samson, so David was on his own.

Tears were streaming down my cheeks as I watched Samson's shivering body. I tried to comfort him, but nothing I did helped. I was also asking myself: Why would LittleBit leave us? But then, dogs do not reason. She did not know she was leaving us, maybe never to return. She was just on a walkabout, following that sensitive nose to wherever it would lead her.

I decided to call the police to see if LittleBit had been found. A dog had been turned in, but the lady on the phone did not think it was LittleBit from my description. "You are welcome to come and see her."

David returned about fifteen minutes later to check in with me, and I told him to go to the police station. As he drove down the road, the phone rang. "Have you lost a dog?"

"Oh my, yes, a little dog—part beagle."

"Where do you live?" I gave our street name.

"Well, we're just one block away." The street was a short distance south of where we lived.

"Oh, how did you find her?"

"Well, she crashed my twins' birthday party."

"I'm so sorry."

He chuckled. "Oh, no. She didn't do any harm. It was quite funny. She came wandering in to join the party. She's quite a cutie and so friendly."

"Yes, we love her to bits."

He chuckled. "She probably smelled the food. She came into the yard and greeted everyone."

"That's our LittleBit. You said it's your twins' birthday today? It's my birthday today too, and you have just given me a wonderful present. Thank you so much."

"Well, I'm glad she had on a name tag. Where did you get it? It's great that it has the telephone number on it. I'd like to get one for my dog."

I gave him as much information as I could remember. As he was telling me the number of the street, David pulled into the driveway. I shouted to him, "LittleBit has been found. She's just on the next street. She's crashed a birthday party."

I gave the address to David, and again thanked the kind father as David raced out of the driveway.

When he returned with LittleBit, I was of two minds—hug her or scold her. Then I realized she wouldn't know why I was telling her off. The last hour seemed like an eternity—my concern for Samson balanced with my concern for Bitty.

The one thing we would have to investigate was how she got out.

That evening David finally talked me into going out for a quick dinner at a local restaurant, insisting I needed a break from all the worry. Samson had settled down and was sleeping, no shivering or panting.

I rushed through dinner, not very hungry, and I wrapped up half of my salmon for Samson. Maybe that would tempt him. All of my lovelies were used to my coming home from dinner out with something in a napkin, but this time it was just for Samson.

That did it. Samson gobbled it up like he had not eaten for days, but then he hadn't. I slept beside him that night at the bottom of the bed—his favorite spot. David and I petted and soothed him when he panted or shivered. Another sleepless night.

The following day with Samson by my side, his eyes fixed on my every movement, I searched the internet to learn about other people's experiences with dogs that had lymphoma and used chemo.

People had reported the same issues Samson was experiencing—the panting alternating with the shivering. Some suggested changing drugs, warned of certain drugs, and so on. Others advocated abandoning chemo altogether. Each story was different. Everyone had such heartache, and every dog was in such pain.

Chapter 17
For the Love of Samson

*I loved you your whole life. I will miss you
the rest of mine.*

The following Monday, we took Samson to our vet to discuss what to do next. Yet, deep down, I believed we had made a decision.

"Can you cut down on the dosage? Can you change the drugs you are giving him?" I asked.

"No, the procedure and drugs are what I know works the best. It would be a waste of time if we gave him something else or less. Yes, he may not get sick, but it will not help long term."

"But we cannot watch him go through another week like this."

"You should have called me. You know you almost lost him."

"We wanted to skip last week, but your replacement vet did not agree." I wanted to add that was why we almost lost him, but it would only vent my anger. It was not going to help Samson.

As Dr. H explained, I felt he would like to escape from the room. It could not be easy for him either to have limited choices, knowing that the only thing you can do could fail. He had admitted that if the chemo was not effective, the lymphoma could come back in months.

"Well, let's not give him the treatment this week. Give him a chance to recover. That will give you both time to think about whether you want to continue with the chemo. It's your choice."

"But as I said before, I don't like either choice. We are being asked to let Samson die or continue to make him suffer or both."

"Yes, I know, but that's all that can be done. It's the same for people. Lymphoma is a horrible cancer."

"Maybe we should try some herbs, something to keep him more comfortable and maybe prolong his life."

"Well, you can talk to Dr. E about that. That's her area."

As we walked out, Samson in David's arms, we felt helpless. It was heart-wrenching for us to watch him shivering and panting. This playful and vibrant dog always had such energy and enthusiasm, and now he was totally debilitated.

It was late August when we decided not to continue with the chemo and met with Dr. E. She specialized in alternative therapies and herbal remedies. She had seen both Samson and Delilah in the past for their annual wellness checkup and Delilah's teeth. We believed she would be helpful and caring.

"So, how much success have you had with herbs in cases like this?" David asked.

"Well, I've had success when herbs have been combined with the chemo."

"So, this is a test case?" I say in a low voice.

"In some ways, yes. He will also be given prednisone. The best that can be done is to keep him healthy and out of distress. Hopefully, that will prolong his life. We'll start him on vitamins and herbs, and I will give you a diet for him that is high in protein and contains only meat or fish and vegetables, and fruit, and no grain."

"Not even rice!"

"Grain feeds cancer cells. That includes rice."

"But I use rice to settle his stomach."

"Use potatoes. It will do the same thing."

Over the following weeks, he was full of energy, playful, and back to our dear Samson Boy. Yet, we both knew that his days were numbered. We did not know when his lymph nodes would swell up again, and although we did not speak of it, it was present in my mind every day.

At times it was difficult to reconcile this decision. Intellectually, I knew we were choosing to let him die, but he was going to die no matter what we did. It was a matter of when and how to keep him as pain-free as possible. Our wanting to hold on to him should not cause him pain and suffering. His well-being was in our hands, and we had to put him first. We would not be putting him first if we continued doing what caused him to suffer but that didn't lessen my heartache.

Samson's appetite returned, and I was kept busy buying the ingredients needed for his diet. I had always cooked for the dogs, so this was not a hardship.

During September and into October, Samson ran and played and enjoyed his time with the girls. He had no difficulty with his new diet, and I fed him three times a day to ensure he did not lose weight. The herbs that we were giving him increased every week or two.

Fortunately, he was not like Delilah when it came to pills. He was so anxious to eat that he never noticed the foreign objects in his food.

At night Sophie cuddled beside Samson, and they continued to sleep together at the foot of our bed.

In September, David got an invitation to attend his grandson's birthday. We decided he would make the trip to England alone. I would stay home with Samson and the girls.

By the time David left on October 25, Samson's lymph nodes had started to swell up again. The drugs and herbs were not working, or they had worked and delayed the inevitable until now. Either way, we knew we were starting the countdown.

When David returned a week later, Samson had done well and was still eating and wanting more and still playing with the girls. He still followed me everywhere, with Sophie tagging right behind.

I said to David, tears in my eyes, "Samson is training Sophie to take his place."

There were still no signs that he was not well, and we were grateful for every day that he was still our Samson boy. That year we had a warm November, and we were all outside. Samson, Sophie, and Bitty were racing around the yard. It was a typical day—a few days before Thanksgiving.

They all raced to the gate, barking at a dog who dared to walk down their street.

"He looks so good and so alive," I said to David, grinning.

"He seems to be doing well."

Four days later, we noticed that Samson's breathing had become labored, and he was zapped of all energy. That night he collapsed at the foot of our bed. His eyes still followed me as I moved around the room, but that was the only life I could see.

On Thursday, he was not interested in food and did not stray from his bed. He barely wagged his tail when I came near. He could not move, and he was struggling to breathe. We had waited too long. He was suffering, but it was so heart-wrenching to say goodbye.

I snuggled beside him on the floor, trying to relax and comfort him, or maybe I was comforting myself. I felt at a loss as to what to do--yet I knew what must be done.

"Elizabeth, we've got to take him...."

"Maybe, she can give him something." Yet, I knew what that something would be.

We drove in silence to the veterinarian clinic. David had called, so they were expecting us. As we entered, we saw Dr. E—now Laura—to our left. "What's happening?"

She looked at my face with tears streaming down and then at Samson. She quickly ushered us into a room. One of the staff came in and put a blanket on the floor. David placed Samson on it as I got down to be with them.

When Dr. E came back in, she looked down at Samson. "Look how good he looks. He hasn't lost any weight. You have done a great job with him."

I know that was meant to comfort us, but it did not.

"What can we do? How can we help him?" I sobbed.

"There's nothing I can do. Look at him. It's time."

As I write this, tears are streaming down my cheeks when I remember the sadness of that day.

David touched Samson's head. "What will happen now?"

"I will give him a shot to make him drowsy. Then I will give him the injection to stop his heart. Have you decided what you want us to do with his body?"

"We haven't talked about it. I buried one of my dogs under a crabapple tree in my first home, and it took me years to sell it because she was buried there. Then I realized she was really buried in my heart."

"It is difficult to move and leave your dog's remains behind. I've buried a dog too, and I've also cremated. I suggest you cremate. When you are ready, you can spread the ashes in his favorite place or not."

While waiting for the first injection, I kept petting Samson and saying, "I'm sorry, sorry, sorry, Samson Boy." Always by my side, I said that when I accidentally stepped on his paw or tripped over him. He would then come to me to lick my hand to tell me everything was okay, but this day he could not.

We both continued to pet him and talk to him, although I didn't hear what we were saying.

The rest is a blur….

The three girls greeted us when we got home. We had no way of telling them about Samson, but maybe they knew. There will always be an empty space that Samson once occupied for David and me and maybe for them too.

Over the following days and weeks, I kept reminding myself that I had three other little dogs to take care of but that could not ease my sorrow. Our girls would fill my days with fun and laughter, but Samson had taken a piece of my heart with him—a piece that would be bound up with his heart forever.

Chapter 18
Delightful Delilah

It came to me that every time I lose a dog, they take a piece of my heart with them. And all the dogs that come into my life give back to me pieces of their heart. If I live long enough, all the components of my heart will be dog, and maybe I will become as generous and loving as they are.

Unknown

I cannot think of anything that brought me closer to tears than when Delilah jumped up beside me, put her head in my lap, her paw over my knee, closed her eyes, and went to sleep. I don't know what I had done to deserve such sheer joy.

At Christmastime, I received a package from Millie. It was a lovely, old book about a dog, signed with love and a thank you from Millie for fostering her and an update on her happy life. It was indeed a match made in heaven.

The following year had begun quietly. All of you who have lost a dog know there is no way to explain the hollowness inside. I spoke of Samson often. I guess to keep him alive. We were trying to settle into having a life without him.

Then on the fourth of January, I noticed that the wart on Delilah's neck was bleeding. We called our vet's office and asked for an emergency appointment. Dr. H was surprised to see us and knew of our losing Samson. He responded to Delilah's lively personality, smiling as she wiggled her bottom and walked around as though she were in charge. Given her age and heart condition, he suggested using a procedure to seal the wound so she would not have to be operated on.

We took her home, and within days, the wound had opened again and was oozing. He told us she could not have an open wound, and it would not heal on its own. It had to be removed.

Again, we faced the scare of the anesthesia, and again I cautioned, "Please use as little as possible."

At the same time, Dr. H decided to remove the enormous fatty tumor on her neck and the one on her backside. There was nothing he could do about the ones under her front arms. They had grown so big and were probably tangled around the muscle. If he tried to remove them, it could leave her disabled.

The day she was operated on I stayed close to the phone, waiting for it to ring. Dr. H called late in the morning and said she had done fine under the anesthesia and experienced no distress.

When we picked her up later that day, she looked like she had run into a buzz saw, but she was still our lovely Delilah. The stitches on her backside were several inches long, but she did not seem to be bothered.

We were told to keep her quiet and not allow her to run up the stairs or jump up or down. She had the operation on Thursday. The following Saturday, the sealed incision on her backside had pulled apart, and the fascia layer was exposed. He had not used stitches, thinking the sealing material would hold.

I quickly called Dr. H—we still had his cell number from our time with Samson. He told us that if he could get someone in the clinic, he would meet us there on Sunday, but he knew he could not. "It looks worse than it really is. Put hot compresses on it and keep her still."

"I just don't know how it happened."

"I'm so sorry. I thought the sealer would hold."

The following Monday, we ran into Dr. H as we entered the clinic. He apologized profusely as we handed over Delilah one more time. Again, she had to go under anesthesia. This time he put in heavy stitches with a drain tube that would have to be removed later. It was hard to keep her down, but we tried. Fortunately, she healed quickly, and again, she was our joyful "wiggle bottom."

Then in April, I noticed a growth on her backside. Again, David convinced the vet's office that we had an emergency. Dr. H said the growth needed to be removed, believing it was cancerous. Again, we faced the cancer scare and the anesthesia with her heart condition. I cautioned, "Use as little anesthesia as possible, please."

Every time we came in with one of the dogs, Dr. H always praised us for bringing our dogs in so quickly. He said he wished more people did that. "I hear too often that the symptoms have been going on for weeks before coming."

I understood that too. Wanting to know and not wanting to know. Hoping and wishing things would change, but they rarely did.

The growth was not cancerous, so we breathed a sigh of relief. Delilah came through the operation and recuperated quickly. She was a strong-willed little lady and did not let anything get her down.

That summer, she spent a lot of time on her bed. When she took a walkabout outside, she was quick to return. The years were catching up with her. That summer, given the information we received when we adopted her, she would be fourteen.

We were delighted we had gotten through the summer without further problems, so we decided to take her for another sonogram to check her heart condition. Such visits were tense for us, never knowing what might be found.

The specialist was pleased that her heart had not deteriorated too much but decided to put her on two medications. We were to start with one and then add the other later. He was a visiting vet that came in from the big city every week, so he didn't have the medication. That was when we got Delilah a card at one of the drugstore chains, so her prescriptions could be discounted.

Once again, Delilah was an expert at finding the pill in her food, no matter how tiny. The problem was that she had never been a "foody" and never relished her food, although she loved treats. Soon after we adopted her, I had given her the nickname "fussy britches."

Anyway, we wrapped meat around it, and sometimes she would swallow it quickly. Other times she would swirl it around in her mouth and then spit out the pill. It soon became a game of finding something we could put the pills in that would fool her. Cheese was the obvious solution, but even then, sometimes out came the pill.

In early October, I found it challenging to get her to eat her meals, so the pills became more of a problem. Then all of a sudden, she came to me asking for food. I could not give her enough. After dinner, she still danced around David asking for treats—reviving her other nickname, "the nagger." Now, she was nagging for anything.

It was early November, and one night she could not go up the stairs, so David carried her. It happened again when she had to come down. Then the next night, while I was petting her, she winced when I touched her. Maybe it was arthritis, or she had hurt her leg. While petting her belly, I found a large lump. It appeared that she had gained some weight because her belly was bulging. I had expected her to gain weight with the increase in food but not a lump.

Again, we took her to Dr. H, who told us she had cancer. He suggested we take her to the same traveling vet for a sonogram to see if the cancer had traveled. After doing the sonogram, that vet gave us some hope and suggested we go back to Dr. H. for an x-ray, even though it was evident that she was filling up with fluid.

When we arrived the following day for the x-ray, Dr. H met us. Delilah was walking around the office, her tail curled up. He could not help but smile.

"Dr. S suggested we bring her to you for x-rays," I said, trying to hold back the tears and not succeeding.

"What are you thinking? There is no way I can operate and remove that tumor. It's huge and three-fourths liquid.

I've read the report and seen the sonogram. An x-ray is just wasting your money."

Tears were streaming down my face, as they are now as I write this. "There's no hope?"

"I'm sorry, but there isn't."

We wrapped her in a blanket, and David carried her out to the car. Neither of us could speak. Time was running out for our lovely, delightful Delilah, our precious Little Dee.

The following two weeks, she slept by me in bed. I held her to me, trying to give her my strength, trying in some way to have her hold on. As I tried to give her my energy, I could feel it draining from me, but I so wanted to ease her suffering.

By day, our Diddle Dee was still active—not as much then as she had been but still very much herself. It was obvious the bulge in her belly kept growing bigger every day. She still came for her pets and cuddles and still managed to nag David about her treats. She never cried out, and not once was there any indication that she was in pain. Our proud Delilah was still the boss of the pack. But her energy level was declining, and the beautiful, feisty spirit we had loved so dearly for so many years was slowly draining away.

We lost our delightful Delilah, our precious Little Dee, a year, almost to the day, after we lost Samson….

The day after Delilah passed away, David dragged me out for a walk, despite the chill in the air. "Remember, we still have two dogs that want to go for walks," he said.

As we arrived near a grocery store, I said to David, "I'm going to go in and get some oranges so we can make some marmalade."

When I walked out of the store, David was talking with a friend of mine. She hugged me and gave me her sympathies. She was a dog lover who had lost several dogs of her own. As we were talking, another friend was walking by and stopped. She could see my red eyes and tears and asked what had happened.

After they left, a woman ringing the Salvation Army bell said, "I overheard your conversation. I know what it's like to lose a pet. I've lost two dogs, a cat, and two birds."

"Oh, I'm so sorry."

"I just can't do it anymore. Every time I lose a pet, a piece of my heart dies. I'm old now, and I need what is left of my heart to keep living."

I didn't know what to say. Her comments surprised me. I always thought I would want to have at least one dog as long as possible, but I understood her heartache.

Chapter 19
Fostering Again

People leave imprints on our lives, shaping who we become in much the same way that a symbol is pressed into the page of a book to tell you who it comes from. Dogs, however, leave paw prints on our lives and our souls, which are as unique as fingerprints in every way.

Ashley Lorenzana

The pleas to foster dogs kept coming during the more than a year we had been nursing Samson and Delilah. Many of them tugged at my heartstrings, but we wanted to give LittleBit and Sophie more of our time. Then, after Samson's passing, we decided to let Delilah live out her life in tranquility, with minimal noise and upheaval—a quiet life.

Losing Samson had affected us deeply. Delilah's passing just a year later devastated both of us, multiplying our grief by more than just one more loss. I knew my healing would take quite a while—how long, I did not know. I also realized that losing our two precious companions within a year was taking a toll on my spirit, essence, and well-being.

How to heal? When would I stop crying? When would the pain in my heart lessen? Those questions kept reeling in my head, but there were no answers. I felt I could not spend my days so sad, and as David often reminded me, "You still have two wonderful doggies to take care of, and they just adore you."

I knew that, but there were two big holes in my heart. I would be doing a chore and would start sobbing again and again. The right side of my body had become riddled with pain from below my breast into my groin—front and back.

In the following month, I visited several doctors in the hope of relieving the pains I was experiencing. The last doctor I met had part of the answer. After telling him my symptoms and his seeing the tears streaming down my cheek as I told him about losing Samson and Delilah, he said to me, "It's all muscle pain brought on by stress. I assure you that you're not dying."

He suggested drugs—pain pills, anti-depressants, steroids, and seeing a psychiatrist. Not liking any of the options, I was in a quandary, but I knew I was the only one who held the answer.

When I lost my first dog, a beagle I nicknamed Boomer, my life forced me to get on with doing what needed to be done. Then one day the river wouldn't stop flowing, tears streaming down my cheeks, my being feeling crushed under the weight of my sorrow. I remember thinking I hadn't taken the time to mourn Boomer. We're supposed to mourn, and for me part of that was being sad and in tears.

I had to give myself permission to have those feelings, which I felt I was being denied. Society has unwritten rules about not crying in public, keeping your feelings buttoned up. People feel helpless and uncomfortable with emotion and shy away, so we learn to keep those emotions hidden and in time they are buried until they are not.

Then there was dear David, who too felt helpless seeing me so sad. He thought that having two other dogs to take care of was a remedy for my sadness. It doesn't work that way. You just can't put your heartache in a box. I had to mourn, and I had to find a place to cry and ache without worrying who I made uncomfortable.

In late February, almost three months after Delilah's passing, our rescue group sent an e-mail asking for foster homes for laboratory beagles—all males, anywhere from 3-4 years old. David was quick to agree when I suggested we foster again. He felt helpless as I mourned our "original two" and although he didn't say it, I believed he thought fostering would help me work through my grief.

In speaking with the volunteer coordinating the intake of these laboratory dogs, we talked about the heartache of losing a dog. I told her the story of the woman outside the grocery store and what she had said.

"Yes, I've heard that before, but there is something else I heard. Every time you take a dog into your life, you get that piece of your heart back."

After listening to her explanation of the challenges of a laboratory foster, I asked for the smallest one of the six for two reasons. LittleBit and Sophie were small dogs and anxious around large ones. A laboratory dog has never walked upstairs, so until they learn to do so, we would have to carry him up and down—a not-so-easy chore for either of us.

The day arrived to pick up Bartley—the name that was given to him by the laboratory before they turned them over to the rescue. Because it was near St. Patrick's Day, all the dogs were given Irish names. When we looked inside the back of the transporter's SUV, I noticed that our foster stood tall on his long, lanky legs, more than 16 inches tall, I was sure, although I never measured him.

He was strikingly handsome with long, floppy ears and black circles around his eyes. He was brown and black—no white and a very long tail.

"I thought we were getting the smallest dog," I said, noticing a smaller dog in the other crate.

"You're to get Bartley. You have a fenced-in yard, and we've been told he is rambunctious and needs one," came the reply from the woman who transported the dogs. She was going to foster the smaller one.

Bartley was a gorgeous boy in need of a loving home. After we got him out of the crate, I hugged him to me, and I could feel his ribs. That was a reminder of the first time we saw Samson. He was definitely a bag of bones. You know the saying that valuable gifts come in small packages. Well, that day, a wonderful gift came in a large package.

There was a directive that we crate the dogs for transport and not stop and let them out of the car because laboratory dogs are skittish. If they hear a sound, they might bolt and get loose. Fortunately, the crate would not fit in our car. Even if it had, I would not have crated him.

I believe that the bonding with us should occur immediately, and a crate is a barrier to touch and smell and hugs and pets. I just had to be careful and hold on tight to him if a door opened for any reason. I also attached a second lead to him and tied it around my headrest.

As was our custom, I wanted him to sit on my lap on the way home so we could begin our bonding with touch—petting and hugging him—and voice—cooing in his ear with a happy lilt in my voice.

Because he was so large, I climbed into the back seat beside him. He was all legs and sprawled out on the seat next to me, but it was not more than a few minutes before he settled in, sniffing around and welcoming the attention.

As I said the name Bartley, I laughed and said to David, "I think we need to change his name."

"Can we do that?"

"Yes, one of the e-mails said we could name him whatever we wanted."

"So, what do you want to name him?"

"I thought that if he had that black eyeliner around his eyes, maybe we would name him Bogey. He does have the eyeliner I imagined, but I'm not sure it fits him."

"Bogey is a good name, but I'm with you. I'm not sure."

On the way home, we took turns suggesting names to each other and finally settled on Bailey.

"It's perfect!" I cried and then cooed in Bailey's ear. "Bailey Boy. Good boy!" He licked my face. I couldn't help but remember Samson. Good Samson Boy!

A belly wrap had been recommended to help housetrain Bailey. Since male dogs lift their legs, unlike Samson, it would keep the furniture and walls from getting sprayed until he got the idea.

Before his arrival, I had ordered two belly wraps online, thinking that he would be a small dog. After seeing him, I knew they would not fit. So, on our way home, we stopped at a pet store to buy larger nappies.

Of course, we had to take him inside to try them on to get the perfect fit. Both leads were attached to him as we got him out of the car. The minute he got out, he was anxious and cowered and unwilling to walk on a lead. We finally coaxed him to walk and got him inside the store.

He was patient, never squirming or pulling away, as we tried on several models and sizes. We finally settled on one model and made our way to the checkout counter.

The ride was about ninety minutes. I was grateful for all that time with Bailey. We used the same method of introducing him to Sophie and LittleBit. It was a quiet beginning—sniffing and tails wagging.

In those first few minutes, Bailey was anxious about coming up the two steps from the mudroom into the kitchen, but the girls showed him the way. Within minutes he was going up and down them, following me in and out of the pantry as I put away groceries we had purchased before picking him up.

David took to Bailey immediately and vice versa. In some ways, I'm sure he reminded David of Samson, and in all ways, he was a charmer. He had a calm demeanor, eager to please, and responded to praise. "Good Bailey Boy!" had his tail whipping back and forth.

"Well, we know he's not housetrained, so we need to limit his space to the kitchen if he has an accident," I suggested to David as we sat down for lunch.

That afternoon I caught Bailey getting ready to squat, just like Samson, no leg lifting, and quickly shooed him outside. He found a spot on the back patio and did a tee-tee. David praised him and rubbed his ears.

LittleBit did not disappoint. As she had done since she arrived, she went over and squatted, lifting her one leg—something she had done since her first day with us. Whenever we praised another dog, she would perform, even if it were just a dribble. Our adorable Bitty.

Bailey repeated this performance two more times that afternoon, and I praised him using a happy voice and clapping, and both of us shouting, "Good Bailey Boy." His excitement about being praised prompted me to say to David, "Maybe he will be easy to train, and we won't need those nappies we bought." I hadn't yet put one on him yet.

David chuckled, "If it keeps him from wearing them, I'm sure he'll do his best."

Bailey was investigating the patio when he noticed the five steps from the patio to the porch. I shouted to David, "Look, he's going up the patio steps."

"Yes, but will he come down?" David said as Bailey got to the top step and turned around, looking at the steps below.

He stood frozen. "I think coming down is going to be a problem. Five steps just seem to be too much. I'm sure he's frightened."

"So, should I carry him down?" David said, walking towards Bailey.

"No, let him figure it out."

It took him about fifteen seconds before he came down the first step. Then, he walked along the step to the other end. Then he went down the next step, traversed that one, and so on. What a bright boy!

"Good Bailey Boy," I yelled, clapping my hands. He came running, wagging his tail and welcoming the pets and hugs I gave him.

That night Bailey came with us to the bottom of the stairs to the second floor.

"So, how are we going to get him upstairs?" David said, looking into Bailey's eyes and then at me.

"It was suggested that we throw popcorn on the steps to coax him. I don't want to give him corn—even popped. It will also depend on how motivated he is by food. He may be another Delilah. I'll get some kibble."

I tossed the kibble on the steps. Bailey went up three steps and then came down. He did this several times but was unwilling to go any farther. The kibble was still on the steps.

He was not going up the entire flight the first night, nor could we expect that, so David carried him up.

Walking into the bedroom, I noticed the crate David had brought up from the garage.

"Well, I guess we have to set up the crate."

Many in the rescue group were now advocating crating foster dogs and crate training. A crate-trained dog attracts potential adopters who want crate-trained dogs. This had not been true in the past, but things had changed since the last time we fostered.

For me, crating should be a short-term solution and not used to replace training or be a continual home for a dog, especially all day. I advocate putting a dog in a crate only when he might attack another dog like Jake, or if the dog is destructive--chewing everything in sight and possibly eating something that can harm him. That was like Samson when we first got him. Once the chewing phase is over, or the dog is housetrained, and the room has been made free of anything that could harm him, etc., the crate can be put away. Other dog companions disagree. That's their choice.

That night we put him in a crate with a blanket, thinking he might be more comfortable since that was his history. Bailey accepted the crating without a complaint. All of us slept soundly, and the following morning David got him up and took him out, leaving the girls and me to sleep. This was the same routine with Samson and Delilah when we lived in New York. The boys went out and played, and the girls snuggled down.

I found time throughout the next day to pet and hug Bailey between my writing and the gardening and general chores. He was so darn cute and lovable, and anytime he saw either of us near, he came running.

He was an adorable floppy-eared dog, all legs, moving quickly here and there. What fun!

Chapter 20
Bailey Boy

Near this spot
Are deposited the Remains of one
Who possessed Beauty without Vanity,
Strength without Insolence,
Courage without Ferocity,
And all the Virtues of Man
Without his Vices

Lord Byron to Boatswain, a dog

Our next step was getting Bailey on a routine. It's worth repeating: Dogs are creatures of habit, so we wanted to put things in place that would help with the housetraining. We thought this would be more difficult since he had probably spent most of his day in a crate or confined, unable to go whenever he wished.

The first step to housetraining was David taking Bailey outside when he got up in the morning. He also had the opportunity to bond with Bailey on his own.

We then took all the dogs out again after breakfast, mid-day, after dinner, and before we went to sleep, praising all the dogs when they performed. No accidents on that day.

In the evening, Bailey decided that he liked the loveseat in the library, where we all gathered to read or watch television. I could not help but chuckle when I saw his long legs hanging over the edge.

"Well, should we allow him on the loveseat? I can put a blanket on it and let him flake out there, or should we insist he go on his bed?"

"Let's try to keep him on the bed for NOW!"

That night there was the challenge of getting him up the stairs again. He watched the girls race up, but he still would not budge, so David carried him again. The following day Sophie and LittleBit raced down the steps while Bailey looked on. We tried to coax him, but he was not going to move. He needed another ride.

That night, he started to go up the steps, got to step four, and turned around as if to say, "I can't do this." We tried to coax him the rest of the way, but he was still not ready.

The following morning, he started going down the steps but stopped after a few. I said to David, "Look down at those steps. They have to be frightening to a dog that has never gone down any steps before. He's doing fine for now."

David chuckled, "I'm going to start charging him for these rides."

On day four, Bailey decided to follow the girls down the stairs. He went down a few steps and then started tumbling down the rest, chin first, his long legs sprawled out at the sides. It was quite funny, but poor Bailey. As I raced down the steps after him to make sure he was OK, he got up and ran after the girls without missing a beat.

From that day forward, he came into the house, ran through the kitchen, and up the stairs to the second floor and then down again. He did this repeatedly, almost like a game, as if to show us he could do it.

As we did every evening, we went into the library. We called Bailey to his bed, but when we turned our heads, he would jump up on the loveseat and snuggle down. If we left him there, in a few minutes, he was asleep. Our boy had a busy day.

After calling Bailey to his bed day after day and finding him on the loveseat, I said to David. "If that's the worst thing he does in our home, we can live with it, can't we? Secretly, I'm hoping his forever family will feel the same way."

As all dog lovers know, it is hard to deny dogs certain pleasures, certain creature comforts. Bailey was no exception. It was also difficult to imagine what he might have endured during the previous three years, living in a cage with little opportunity to go outside, possibly no hugs or pets, and denied who knows what else. Or maybe at the lab one of the researchers liked dogs and did give him pets, but still, he was in that cage.

Within a week, we both concluded that Bailey was one of our easiest fosters. We were convinced on the fourth day that he was housetrained. No accidents, and when he went outside, he performed first thing.

This happened without any treats—just pets, hugs, hand-clapping, and praise. We only used treats to get Bailey to sit around David with the girls, learning not to take from the other dogs. Other times he sat without a treat and came when called.

David and I could not help thinking about Samson boy when we watched Bailey strut around the driveway and garden. Samson had always pranced with such pride, and Bailey did the same. Also, like Samson, he had luscious, velvety ears that I loved to bury my face in. I just hoped Samson wasn't jealous as he watched from above.

Bailey would come running at the sound of my voice, and I hugged him to bits. In the evening, before we put him to bed, he and I played tug-of-war with one of the girls' toys. David and I also played "dog in the middle" like we had with Samson and many of the high-energy fosters.

During the second week, we decided to forgo the crate and let him sleep on his bed on David's side. The first night we covered him, and he tossed the cover off. The minute we turned off the light, he settled down and went to sleep and slept through the night. We kept the room dark, so he did not stir until he saw the light.

The following week he started cuddling under the blanket we left on his bed, tossing it over his head, just as Samson used to do. He had finally made another step to ultimate doggie comfort.

Within a few weeks Bailey had gained some weight and his legs were stronger. Fortunately, he wasn't debilitated like sweet Bonnie. He hadn't birthed litter after litter. He was also taller and about seven pounds heavier than LittleBit and about twelve pounds heavier than Sophie.

Whereas LittleBit would roughhouse in play, Sophie was a sweet, gentle, low-keyed dog. She would cry out when Bailey jumped on her or tackled her in play. It was his height and weight that frightened her. We called a time-out when Bailey got too rambunctious. Then he would come running for attention.

The next three weeks were filled with days of laughter with Bailey's antics. I wish I had a penny for every time I said to him, "You're such a good boy."

Walking him was a lot of fun and very easy. He pranced along, never pulling, and we credited the girls for showing him not to be afraid of life outside our home and yard. Before he came to us, we heard stories that he would be a problem and needed to have a fenced-in yard. He never went to the gate or even near the fence or tried to escape. He was not interested in being anywhere but with our two girls and us.

A dog that had been denied a comfy doggie life for three years, with no hugs and pets, wanted to stay close by. Maybe because he was used to being confined and not roaming the streets for food, he had no inclination to escape. Maybe because he was content. Maybe.

It was also during this time we decided to abandon the leader collar with LittleBit. She held the distinction, at least up until then, as the only dog who fussed about it.

She was now older and did not charge out as quickly as she had, so she wasn't pulling but walking by our side. We wanted her to have more fun and exercise during the walks. She was such a wonderful dog, never giving us any problems from the beginning, and we loved to see her so happy and carefree.

I remember that often people thought Samson was a girl and Delilah a boy. One day in Central Park, a little boy called Samson "she" and Delilah "he."

I asked him, "Why do you think that's a boy (pointing to Delilah) and that's a girl (pointing to Samson)?"

From the mouth of babes, he replied. "Because that's a blue collar (Delilah's turquoise one), and that's a pink one (Samson's red one)." Funny, but the colors were not picked because of their gender; they were all the vendor had to sell us that fit.

We decided that because of LittleBit's wide stance and hang-dog look, people always thought she was a boy. I must admit she reminded me of a short, little man, something like Charlie Chaplin. All she needed was a cane. So cute! So wonderful!

With the extended lead, most of the time, she did not pull, so we opted for a vest. It tugged at her broad chest and not her back, and it was bright pink.

I chuckled as I put the vest on her, "Maybe if people see the pink color, they won't call her a boy." Of course, LittleBit didn't care, as long as they fussed over her.

Chapter 21
Bailey Finds a Home—Well, Sort of....

"The love of a dog is a pure thing. He gives you a trust which is total. You must not betray it."
Michel Houellebecq

Sophie didn't even have a year with Samson, and LittleBit barely two years. Both had bonded with him, playing with our dear boy at every opportunity. LittleBit and Sophie were now playing with Bailey with abandon. Such joy to see them so engaged and happy.

In that time LittleBit had never changed her joyful ways, her swagger, and love of toys, just like Samson. One of my favorite pictures of her is on a loveseat with about twenty toys scattered around her. My love for her swelled up day after day, almost making my heart burst.

Sophie, as Samson had done, still followed me everywhere. He had trained her well. Her sweet and gentle ways took my breath away. I always felt she needed care and attention—so much more than our independent LittleBit.

At other times Sophie was by David's side, and he cherished her as he did LittleBit. Bailey was giving us a gift. He was a reminder of Samson, and he was bringing us joy.

The description of Bailey that I wrote for the rescue group's website convinced a mother with a three-year-old daughter that Bailey was the one. The woman's parents had a beagle that recently passed away—a dog the little girl had played with and missed.

Bailey got her attention because she said he was too good to be true, and indeed for us, he was. He was heaven-sent—easy to train, fun and funny, and with a gentle, easy-going temperament.

During the telephone conversation, the mother told me the daughter was excited about having a dog. They had gone out and bought toys for Bailey and were anxiously awaiting his arrival.

The adopter and I spoke again, and she told me that her daughter was sleeping with Bailey's new nametag under her pillow. I could not help but smile and was delighted that Bailey's new family was so excited.

Although we both believed he was a wonderful dog and for us easy to love, we knew it was best to give him up. I could say he was just too much of a dog for our two little girls, playing rough at times, although not knowingly.

Then there was the "me" factor. I wasn't ready. Although Bailey helped ease my sorrow, my heart still ached—too much to think about adopting another dog. Eventually, we decided the pack should remain at two.

The following day we drove him about an hour south to meet his new family. I asked the mother to bring the little girl, but she wanted to surprise her daughter. We thought that was an odd decision as the girl knew she was getting a dog. The mother was denying the girl the first opportunity to bond with Bailey. I couldn't help but wonder why, but I couldn't demand she bring her.

We arrived at the meeting place and got Bailey out of the car. We wanted to give him a chance to sniff around and do whatever before he made another journey. A car pulled up, and the adopter and a man we assumed was her husband got out of the car. Neither greeted Bailey with the exuberance I expected.

Now, I must tell you, if you haven't already noticed, I am a dog lover in all capital letters. In fact, many years ago, a woman called me besotted as I greeted her dog. I also know I have high standards for an adopter, which I have no difficulty admitting.

But, that aside, some kind of greeting to Bailey was definitely warranted. I suggested that she take the lead and walk with me. She ignored me, and the Mr. stooped down to pet Bailey and then took the lead.

As we walked, I chatted about Bailey, and he nodded. When we returned to where she and David were standing, I asked what she thought.

"Well, he's a beautiful dog and seems so mild-mannered."

I admit I was expecting her to get down and pet him, love him up, and show him some affection. Maybe she was getting a dog to keep her daughter entertained. Then, I thought, "She's not going to go ga-ga over a dog like you do, Elizabeth, and that's OK, isn't it? The dog is for her daughter, not her."

Then I stopped my mind. Bailey would be living with all of them.

I stood there at a loss about what to do, regretting that we were giving him up and wondering if we were doing the right thing. It was so hard to make a snap decision, and I can't point to anything definite—once again, just something inside me.

I kept asking myself, "Where is the woman I talked with?" So, after speaking at length about the wonders of Bailey, I finally asked, "So, do you still want him?"

She said, "Oh, yes, my little girl will be so happy."

They put Bailey into their car. As we drove away, I took one last look at "sweet Bailey boy."

"She's so different from the person I spoke with on the phone. She was so excited," I said to David with tears in my eyes.

"It's hard to give him up."

"The home visitor expressed some concern that the daughter frightened her dog, but that concern was dismissed because her dog is a nervous one."

"So, what can we do?"

"I guess just wait. Bailey is resilient, not like Bonnie and Bella. He'll be able to handle whatever, but.... You know, over the years, when I have denied my concerns, I have regretted it. I hope this will not be another one of those days that I will regret."

"I told her she should have brought her daughter," said David.

"What did she say?"

"She just ignored me."

"Well, she told me on the phone she wanted to surprise her. I just don't understand."

We could not pinpoint anything concrete that said she should not adopt him, but something was gnawing at both of us.

Fostering brought us such joy, but sending Bailey on his way with concerns and doubts had made us anxious once again. I would never forget what Bonnie had experienced and Bella's adoption. We wanted to do what was best for our foster dogs, and we did not always know what that was in those few minutes.

The volunteers of rescue groups are dedicated to rescuing dogs and finding them a forever home with all the love and joy they would want for themselves. All the hours everyone invests into their well-being are a gift they give these dogs. And no matter how much time and effort, we had become too aware that not all adoptions stick for so many different reasons. And although I didn't want Bailey's life upended, I believed it would be.

Chapter 22
A Puppy—Oh my!

Enthusiastic greetings rock my world.
Walking through the door.
Tails wagging and heartbeats at my feet.

Again, you guessed it, there was an e-mail asking us to foster a three-year-old female dog. Then a few seconds later, another e-mail announcing there were seven more laboratory beagle puppies to be fostered and several other adult dogs.

David and I talked it over and decided we would take a female adult or puppy and even said we would take both if there were a shortage of homes. After it was all sorted out, we were given a twelve-week-old female puppy.

When we met the transport, there was our foster, plus another tiny female and a bigger male puppy—all of them adorable, of course. Our foster was so tiny, long and lean, with long ears. I was convinced her face would never grow into those ears. Looking at her and then wrapping her in my arms brought tears to my eyes.

Both our foster and the male in the car had cherry eyes. They had been born with cherry eyes, but the laboratory never did anything about that. No reason to do so. The cherry eye is often called the "third eyelid," a red mass resembling a cherry pit in the corner of the eye.

Typically, after the dogs are used and abused in laboratories, they are euthanized. They don't want it to be known they are using dogs for their experiments. Once again, the rescue group talked the laboratory into giving these puppies a chance at life.

She was to be spayed and her eye operated on while in our care. Then it would be a month or more before she could be adopted.

I cuddled her next to me as David drove home. She was so soft. I couldn't stop snuggling that sweet little bundle.

"So, what are we going to name her?" I said to David.

"We get to name another dog?"

"I think we did a good job with Bailey's name."

We tossed around dozens of names, and by the time we arrived home, we had not settled on anything we believed suited her. LittleBit and Sophie greeted her with wagging tails and sniffs. She was just their height, with a much longer body but ten pounds lighter than Sophie and fifteen pounds lighter than LittleBit.

I had not had a puppy since my first dog right out of university, so this would be a new experience. It would be challenging to train her without a name, so I decided to search on the web for dog names. I didn't find a name for this puppy but discovered that Sophie's name was #10 on favorite dog names.

Then it finally hit me. Why not call this little imp Flossie. We always loved that name. For a while, we used it as a nickname for LittleBit, while Delilah's had been Popsy. I suggested Flossie to David, and Flossie it was. It was a perfect name for her. She was a lively little dog with horns somewhere between her ears.

From the first day she arrived in our home, Flossie followed at my heels. I noticed that Sophie did not follow me when Flossie was around. In a few days, I started calling her my "shadow." I said to David that perhaps we should have given her that name.

She was so little and difficult to see at times, so I often tripped over her, saying "sorry, sorry," like I did when I tripped over Samson.

We did not believe her cherry eye was bothersome to her, but we both wondered if it affected her vision. When I threw something for her to chase, she could not seem to follow it with her eyes.

Our first and continual challenge was housetraining. Puppies tee-tee continually, especially after a nap. We decided to go to the pet store to get Flossie nappies that could be washed repeatedly, plus piddle pads. If she squatted, the nappy would save the wooden floors and carpets. We also had to teach her to go in the dirt and grass and not on the cement driveway or garage floor. In the laboratory, her only experience had been with a cement floor.

Again and again, she tee-teed on the driveway, and I would then take her to the dirt. You may recall that I always praised our dogs for going. In this case, because she was so clueless, I took her to Bitty or Sophie's spot and said, "Tee-tee Flossie. Tee-Tee." Clueless!

I laughed thinking of LittleBit when we were training her. We would praise Samson or Delilah when they performed. LittleBit would lift her leg a few inches off the ground and do her thing. She never squatted with both legs. Always one leg was lifted. What a girl!

That bit of theatrics did not work with Flossie, so patience was needed. She also chewed everything in sight and quickly grabbed any piece of stick or wood and chewed on it. I searched the yard looking for anything she might chew that would hurt her. Toys were strewn all over the driveway and yard. I visited pet stores, as I had done with Samson, frequently trying to find something that would interest her besides wood and sticks.

Flossie did have some favorite toys that she chewed, and she loved those that squeaked. She and I had a great time playing fetch. She was just so much fun and had bounds of energy.

Our second challenge would be getting Flossie to go up and down the stairs, especially to our second floor. Like Bailey, she had not mastered that feat, but puppies don't seem to have much fear. Within days she was running up and down the steps, regarding it as playtime.

Nothing could stop Flossie from racing around at full speed when she was outside, often running into Sophie. LittleBit stayed out of her way. Sophie now and then grumbled at her or lunged, chasing her away when she got too rough. Delilah would just bark once. Samson never cared—always up for a game of chase.

After about two weeks, David said, "I think Sophie is mothering Flossie. Her mother would have corrected her, and that's what Sophie is doing with Flossie."

I started paying attention to that and found that to be so. Then Sophie started playing with Flossie, running at lightning speed with the puppy chasing behind. They had become playmates. LittleBit rarely joined in the chase when Flossie was around, often sidelined. Sometimes she barked at them, I believe in protest.

The day finally came for Flossie to be spayed and her cherry eye removed. We were concerned because she was so young—only fourteen weeks old—and so little—weighing about 12 pounds. We had to take her to a veterinary clinic where we did not know the vet or the staff, so we asked to speak to the vet who would be doing the surgery. Flossie was not our dog, but she was in our care, so we just weren't going to hand her over without chatting with him.

The vet blew us both away with his rambling on and on after each question, and we walked out hoping that the unsettled feeling he gave us was not a sign of things to come.

When we picked up Flossie later that day, her eye was oozing, and she looked poorly. The vet repeatedly gave us instructions about the ointment and the pain pills. There were also pills to keep her calm and quiet.

We sifted through what he had said and decided that he had attached the tissue surrounding the third eye to the occipital bone. If that stitching released, the cherry eye would pop out again. She had to wear an Elizabethan collar, and we had to keep her eye lubricated with the ointment.

David especially was convinced that the vet had done nothing to correct Flossie's eye. We could still see a cherry. In time we would know. The cutest and yet irritating thing about the Elizabethan collar was that because Flossie walked right at my heels, like Sophie and Samson before her, the cone bumped into the back of my legs when I stopped because she was so close.

She did not understand that her collar projected about four inches from the end of her nose. I must say the hard edge of that plastic hurt quite a bit. Within a week, I noticed black and blue marks all over the backs of my legs. Of course, I could not help but laugh. She was just so adorable.

The weekend after her operation, we got a call from Bailey's adoption counselor. "Can you foster Bailey again?" She explained that things had not worked out, and he had to be removed from the home.

Why did we have to be right about this adoption?

"I would love to take Bailey back, but I don't think we can do it. Flossie has had her eye operated on and needs a quiet life. Bailey is a wonderful dog but with lots of energy, and he's so big, and she's so small."

It was hard for me not to take him back, so I added, "If you can't find another home, let me know. We'll make it work."

I did not get a call, but I did receive an e-mail from one of my favorite ladies in our organization who was in charge of adoptions. Her heart was as big as the moon.

She had picked up Bailey at the adopter's home and found the little girl pounding on him with her toys. Bailey was just sitting there, and the mother had said nothing to the girl.

The volunteer whisked Bailey away, no words spoken. She reported that he sat down in the back of the car—no problems. "He's as wonderful as you said he is.

He's now with a young couple that just loves him. They would like to talk to you. Can you do that?"

I agreed and had a great conversation with both about Bailey's antics. We laughed and chatted, and I could hear the joy in their voices. He was most loved and appreciated for the glorious spirit he possessed. Sweet Bailey Boy!

A fantastic outcome for Bailey, but once again, so disheartened at how he was treated in that first home. I cannot say enough, "Some people just shouldn't have a dog!" Unfortunately, there is no sure formula to weed out the undesirables.

Chapter 23
Flossie

"When your children are teenagers, it's important to have a dog so that someone in the house is happy to see you."
Nora Ephron

About two weeks after the surgery, Flossie still had the red bump. "That operation didn't work. The cherry is still there," David grumbled one morning as we put the ointment in her eye.

He said what I was thinking, so we took her back to the vet for a checkup. He said the eyelid was still attached. It would take a while longer for the cherry to disappear.

Several months before fostering Flossie, I agreed to facilitate a workshop in another state. I would be gone almost six days. I was going to cancel, but David insisted he would be fine with the dogs. LittleBit and Sophie were so easy, and the little munchkin was so loveable.

A few days before I left, we noticed the eye had improved slightly and very little of the red swelling was showing. Hallelujah! Maybe the vet was right.

I called home every day, but on the third day, I could tell David was upset. "The cherry eye is back."

"Are you sure?"

"Yes, I'm sure! I can see it."

"Well, I guess we can take her back to find out for sure, but I don't think we want to do that. Wait until I get home. I'll see if we can go somewhere else."

When I arrived home late that Friday evening, I was so sad that indeed the cherry eye had returned. I spoke with someone in our rescue group. I sent pictures to have another vet confirm that we were correct.

Three weeks later it was decided we would take her to a vet who would put the third eyelid in a pocket and not attach it to the bone. He had previously adopted one of our dogs and would not charge for the operation. We are grateful for angels.

Again, Flossie would have to endure what had to be unbearable pain to her eye, but our main concern was whether the operation would correct the problem. We were assured it was the right approach, so we delivered her to one of our volunteers who would transport her south.

We picked her up later that day, and she was her cute perky self, but again her eye looked like she had been in a fight. This time there were drops for her eyes, pain pills, and no Elizabethan collar.

After the first operation, she had been very nervous when we tried to get the ointment on her eyelids so it would be absorbed into the eye. The eye drops presented another challenge.

"I'm sure she's afraid that whatever we are doing about that eye will hurt," I said to David as he held her and I squeezed the bottle. Again and again, we tried to get a drop to land in her eye. Over ninety percent of the time one of us missed, and it landed on her nose, head, my hand, chair, whatever.

We decided that one of us should rub the top of her head, trying to get her to relax, hoping she would close her eyes, even fall asleep, and then one of us would squeeze the bottle. She then got to the point where she could smell the bottle or feel my hand near her eye, and she would open her eyes.

One thing was confirmed—she was a bright little girl and she was winning this battle, but we persevered. Eventually, we had to get another bottle of drops so we could continue the treatment.

Now, I know what my mother felt when I resisted her attempts to put drops in my eyes.

The day came when I was asked to take some pictures of Flossie and do a write-up for the rescue website. She had to be put up for adoption. It was time. She had been with us for over two months, so it was easy to share her quirks and endearing qualities. It wasn't so easy to let her go.

A few days after the first pictures and write-up were on the website, I got a call. A young woman in New York City wanted to adopt Flossie. She was an attorney who worked one or two days per week in her home. She also had a friend who had a dog that Flossie could play with in the country on the weekend. Hmmm.

There was concern from one of our volunteers about a dog living in New York City. I did not share that concern—after all Samson and Delilah had started their lives with us in that same city. But I also knew that there were two of us to walk and take care of them. If there were problems with the Board, if she owned or if she rented, with the management company or owner, what would she do? Abandon the dog?

Then, Flossie as a young pup had to be considered. She needed training and in time lots of exercise. Also, wanting a dog because her friend had a dog and so the two dogs could play together was not reassuring. That one bit of information did not assure me that she would be a responsible human companion for adorable Flossie.

Arrangements were made for a home visit. The goals were to see her space and to make sure she knew the challenges of having a dog in the city. Then we would all discuss whether this was a good match.

Now, you might be asking, "Didn't you want to get her adopted?" and "Didn't you want to adopt her?" Yes, of course, I did in some ways. The bonds were so strong, not only because of the months we had spent together, but because of how fragile and vulnerable she seemed to be. I thought about it again and again, but every time I mentioned adopting her to David, he did not say emphatically, "Yes, we should," as he had done with Samson, Delilah, LittleBit, and Sophie.

There was our pack to consider. Flossie was following me everywhere and was rarely out of my sight. Initially, she stayed outside with LittleBit and Sophie, but more and more she wanted to be beside me. It was also becoming clear that Flossie should not be the only dog, and most definitely she should not be alone all day. I expressed this to the adoption counselor who was involved with the New York adopter. The proposed adoption with the young attorney in New York was nixed.

Over the next few weeks, the thought, "I'm not ready to have another dog," kept swirling around in the back of my mind. It was also obvious that LittleBit had not bonded with Flossie the way she had with Samson and now Sophie. Sophie seemed to be neutral—take her or leave her.

Also, puppies are easy to get adopted, just like the female dogs one to three years old. We had made a pact early on that we would only adopt an older dog or one that couldn't get adopted. Sophie was just over three it was assumed, so she could be considered an exception, but in hindsight it was fortuitous. But we were of one mind about adopting an older dog.

We knew that would limit our adopting another dog, but it was what we wanted to do. LittleBit, we had to adopt. She was meant to be ours, no matter her age. Sophie came into our home, and it was like she was always there—a happy pack.

When I stepped back and looked at the idea of adopting Flossie, if this decision were so difficult, it was not meant to be. I had to let her go.

Chapter 24
Ki-Ann or Something Like That

She talks and groans and even sighs
To rescue her was more than wise
Always flitting here and there
Now she lives without a care

Her name was Ki-Ann, or Kiah, or something like that. No one was sure, even the woman surrendering her. We were asked to foster her while Flossie was still with us because they had no other foster home.

When I spoke with the foster director, I discovered that Ki-Ann lived about five blocks away from our home. I decided that if we were going to take on a second foster, with Flossie still a challenge, I needed to know more.

The next day David and I were returning from a shopping trip. I suggested that we call on Ki-Ann's guardian and see the situation. A last-minute decision, with no telephone number but an address, we arrived on the doorstep. I was delighted when I knocked on the door and someone was home. I explained my purpose for the visit and was invited in.

The minute I entered it was obvious Ki-Ann needed to get out of there. Immediately, she ran to the corner of the room to hide. I could see that most of the hair down her back was missing, and I could smell a definite odor. I went over to her, trying to engage her, but there was no response.

The woman who was surrendering her had taken Ki-Ann from her nephew who had been living in a car and apparently harming the dog. I was told Ki-Ann was afraid of people—especially men.

The woman sighed, "She's a really nice dog, but I just can't take care of two dogs." There was a fluffy dog also in the room who wasn't friendly.

After spending about half an hour with Ki-Ann and her guardian and meeting other family members, I walked away upset that this dog was suffering so. David had been waiting in the car—believing that both of us in the house might be overwhelming. I explained the situation to him and what I had observed.

"So, we're going to foster her?"

"I'm not sure. It's a very sad situation, and she's a lovely dog. I got her to let me pet her, and she's very friendly with the woman's son, although she's not supposed to like men."

"So, there is hope for me?"

"Time will tell."

After a lengthy discussion, it was obvious we were hesitant about taking her. We have learned from Millie and Sallie that it was difficult to have two dogs if both were time-consuming and had issues, such as training, being skittish.... They took up a lot of time and energy and some things may not get addressed quickly enough. It also takes longer to get certain issues resolved—issues that might take less time if we could focus on one dog only.

I informed the foster director of our decision not to foster until Flossie was adopted. So, we were surprised when a volunteer who had taken Ki-Ann to be vetted arrived at our door late on a Friday with Ki-Ann in tow. We were told she had a flea allergy and hookworm, and there was no foster home for her.

The plea, "Can you take her, at least for a little while?"

"I know she has to get out of her situation, but…."

The volunteer had three dogs, including a foster as well, so she didn't want to take her.

"Elizabeth, we had no choice but to take her," said the volunteer. "She wanted Ki-Ann gone asap. We all know you're one of our best. One of a few willing to take two. The vet took care of her fleas, so there should not be a problem. The hookworm…… Well, that can be a problem since it's highly contagious."

LittleBit, Sophie, and Flossie were in the house. While the volunteer and I were talking, David came from the garage knowing nothing of the situation. Ki-Ann immediately began barking at him and running in circles—almost at hyper speed. That shook David, but he kept calling her to him. She would come close and then run away. He called her again and again, and each time she ran away.

We were both concerned about taking her in with three dogs—one being a puppy—and hookworm that was contagious. We would have to be careful that we pick up every speck of her doo-doo, so our dogs would not become infected. After several calls to foster volunteers, it was confirmed that there was still no foster home available, so we agreed to keep her for the weekend.

I was given instructions about the hookworm medication and how to treat the fleas, plus there was bathing shampoo that would ease the itch and hopefully clear up the scabs so her hair would regrow on her back. We brought LittleBit, Sophie, and Flossie outside to meet her. The greetings were uneventful and the volunteer left, wishing us the best.

Ki-Ann had a gorgeous face with a mixture of deep rust brown and charcoal black fur with very little white markings. Most beagles have a "grab your soul and heart" eyes, and Ki-Ann was no exception.

It was summer time so we put a bed in the sunroom with some toys and water. Ki-Ann would spend that night there to make sure the fleas were killed before allowing her to come into the kitchen.

She was an easy dog—right from the beginning with the exception of running away from David. He tried again and again, and although she was still skittish, there were some sparks of hope now and then.

Over the weekend we decided that we would continue to foster her. Still no foster home available. In fact, David even mentioned keeping her—as a forever dog. As I have said, he decides quickly. I was still not there. My heart belonged to Flossie and Delilah and Samson, and our two little girls.

It was Tuesday afternoon. Ki-Ann had been with us almost three full days. I was working in the garden, and the dogs were out and about enjoying the sights and sounds and smells of the outdoors.

I opened the gate to go out to the front garden. Before doing so, I made sure all the dogs were in the back garden by the garage. The minute Flossie heard the gate and saw me, she came running with Ki-Ann right behind her.

I tried to close the gate, but it was too late. Ki-Ann escaped, and as I tried to grab her, Flossie escaped too. I screamed for David who came running. It happened so fast. I was in shock. Ki-Ann was half-way down the street when David caught Flossie.

Running down the street I saw four people turning the corner. I yelled at them to catch her. The two young men took off after her, and the two women walked towards me. I explained the situation as a neighbor came from her yard and joined the chase.

As we turned the corner, I could see the men in the distance but not Ki-Ann. For the next half-hour the two women, my neighbor, and I walked around the town trying to find Ki-Ann.

David finally picked me up in the car, and we started driving around to the other side of town, across a bridge with an underpass below. I spotted the two men, and they reported they had seen Ki-Ann but in no way would she come to them. She was just too fast to catch and too skittish.

A few seconds later, we saw her running across the road. The men jumped in our car, and we drove in the direction she was running but could not see her. They got out of the car and raced on foot while we drove around the block.

We continued to drive around, asking everyone we saw if they had seen a beagle. While doing so, we met a couple out for a walk. The woman was so concerned she joined in the search with her car. At about the hour mark—still no Ki-Ann spotted—I called three friends to help in the search.

I knew the sister of the woman who surrendered Ki-Ann and called her for the phone number, thinking the dog might return there. She told me that her husband thought he had spotted Ki-Ann in the area we were looking and would also join in the search. For the next two hours, we all drove around that neighborhood but still no Ki-Ann.

We returned home to take care of our three—it was now dark. Feeling so responsible, I went out by myself for another couple of hours, into the early morning. I was crushed. How were we ever going to get her back? My one friend assured me that Ki-Ann would find a safe place for the night, and we would have a better chance of seeing her in the daylight.

One of the men who was part of the search asked, "What kind of dog?"

"A beagle."

"Beagles don't get lost. They always return home."

Knowing she had probably not considered our home her home yet, I drove to her old home before retiring for the night. There were no signs of her. What I had feared had happened and in an instant.

That night I could not sleep remembering that several of our foster homes have had dogs that escaped. One dog was missing for over two months. She was continually spotted but because like Ki-Ann, she had not been socialized, she would run away. Traps were put out with food where she was sighted. The volunteers in that area never gave up, determined to find her. Eventually she was caught. I did not want this for Ki-Ann. I had to find her.

At the break of daylight, I was up, dressed, driving around. I returned about an hour later to get a cup of tea and check in. David joined me in the search, and as we were driving around, I called the woman's sister again to thank her for her husband's help and to know if she had heard from her sister.

Immediately, she told me that Ki-Ann was at her sister's house. She was sitting across the street, and they were having difficulty getting her inside. We were just a few blocks away, so we raced over. We did not see Ki-Ann outside, so I knocked on the door. Ki-Ann was inside and upstairs with the children.

I charged up the stairs and hugged her to me. I apologized for my carelessness and assured them this would not happen again. Then, I picked up Ki-Ann in my arms and carried her to the car. David greeted us, and we hugged and petted her, cooing in her ears.

That seemed to be a turning point for Ki-Ann. From the moment she returned to our home, she was different. She came for belly rubs, seemed more relaxed, and within hours was coming to David for pets. What clicked we had no way of knowing, but something told her she was safe.

Chapter 25
Saying Goodbye and Hello

Smooshed-in face, soulful eyes.
Dances around me with joy.
Takes my breath away
Mending my heart every day

Ki-Ann became a blessing to us in many ways. After her run-away escapade, she became a stay-at-home girl, always by our sides. Flossie and Ki-Ann played and cuddled together, and Ki-Ann soon became the little one's puppy sitter.

When we left to go shopping or to the theater or dinner, we put them together on the three-season porch, and LittleBit and Sophie were in the kitchen. Ki-Ann kept Flossie entertained and drained her of her surplus energy.

In the meantime, Flossie's eye seemed to be healing, although the cherry was still visible. The drops continued to be a struggle, but she was a happy little girl. At night she cuddled with me in bed. I just could not resist having her beside me. She was such a gentle soul with a little pair of horns. Ki-Ann cuddled next to Sophie snuggled at my feet as she had done with Samson by her side. Bitty snored next to David.

Ki-Ann had been with us for about a week when we got a call. A couple wanted to adopt one of the senior beagles from the rescue group that was about ten years old and a younger dog at the same time. They had chosen Flossie.

The couple had adopted an older dog before and thought the pain would not be as great if they had another dog when the older one passed. How could I tell them it wouldn't matter, but then they would have to learn that in time, but hopefully not too soon.

Meanwhile, Ki-Ann had become comfortable with both of us, but she was still very hesitant with strangers, especially men. One day a worker arrived with a hat on. He was over six-feet tall and wore glasses. Ki-Ann never stopped barking until we removed her from the room.

When I was asked to do the write-up for the website about Ki-Ann, I decided I needed to do something about the spelling of her name. When I said her name, I would think of cayenne pepper. Her russet color was redder than brown, so I thought the spelling of C-A-Y-E-N-N-E was perfect for her. I guess that's why I had nicknamed her Pepper, so Cayenne it was.

Before Cayenne's story was on the web, I got a call from an adoption counselor. She had potential adopters for her. They had an older dog—Miss Bee, thirteen years old. The Mrs. wanted to add a dog to the pack before the other one passed. Two adopters in a row with the same plan, wanting to have a second dog to ease the pain.

The husband was not so sure, and I understood his concerns. A younger dog can be a little much for an older, calm dog. At the same time, a young dog can breathe life into an older dog. I remember my dog Autumn cuddling next to Snuffy, keeping her warm, until she died at almost nineteen. I always felt Autumn kept Snuffy alive for that long.

I spoke at length with the wife about Cayenne being hesitant with men. Miss Bee had some of the same problems with men when they had first adopted her, so they both knew to be patient and were not deterred from adopting her.

She explained that people had told her not to adopt a dog while Miss Bee was still living, so she was not sure what to do and asked me about my thoughts.

"I cannot give you any advice there. Everyone processes loss differently. I will tell you that for me having another dog did not make the loss any easier, and we had two. It probably will not lessen the hurt you feel. At the same time, you will still have someone to fuss over.

"You need to do what is best for Miss Bee. She should be your only concern. How do you want her to spend her last days? Will it be good for her to have a friend by her side for whatever time she has left? I think Miss Bee meeting Cayenne will help you both know what to do."

Two days later I received a second call from the adoption counselor that the adopters who were interested in Flossie were now interested in Cayenne. They had seen her pictures and story on the web.

"There's already a couple interested in Cayenne, but would they be interested in adopting both Cayenne and Flossie? They get along so wonderfully."

"No. Remember they want a senior dog and a much younger one."

"And I would never want to stop a senior dog from getting adopted. At the same time, I think it's best they stick with Flossie. They will love her. I have no doubt."

I made arrangements with the adoption counselor to have the couple visit to meet Flossie. They were going to pick up Starr, the senior beagle, and bring her with them so the two could meet.

The next day I got a call that the other couple who wanted to adopt Cayenne wanted to visit the weekend before Flossie's adopters. It was clear—one way or another, we were going to have to say goodbye to these two dogs, possibly within days or even a week.

Introducing Cayenne to Miss Bee and her potential adopters was going to take some orchestrating because of Flossie. She would upend Cayenne, so we kept her and our Sophie and LittleBit out of sight. When the visitors arrived, I went outside and met Miss Bee. I almost burst into tears. Miss Bee was a chubby, shorter legged version of Delilah.

Because Cayenne was skittish, I asked them to bring some clothing to help with the introduction. They arrived with two pieces of clothing and a toy for Cayenne. David ushered them into the one parlor while I took the clothes and toy out to Cayenne who was in the kitchen. I returned to talk about Cayenne and answer their questions.

Then I suggested that the husband step into the other parlor. I wanted to introduce Cayenne first to the wife and Miss Bee before meeting the husband. I thought this best since I was not sure how Cayenne would respond to him, and I thought Miss Bee should meet Cayenne first. The introduction went wonderfully with Miss Bee and the wife, and immediately Cayenne had captured the woman's heart.

After about five minutes, I took Cayenne into the second parlor to meet the husband. Fortunately, she did not bark at the strange man. Within minutes he was petting her, and she was enjoying him. She had come a long away, probably due to David's tenderness and time spent with her.

Miss Bee's guardians wanted to adopt Cayenne, but they could not take her that very day. They were going on vacation the following week and did not want to put her in a shelter a few days after adopting her. We agreed to keep her two more weeks, which was not normal protocol, but we believed this would be a wonderful home for sweet, darling Cayenne.

It was a sunny beautiful day when Flossie's adopters arrived, and she greeted them with her usual vim and vigor. I explained about her cherry eye. It was still there somewhat, but there had been much improvement over the previous two weeks. Starr, the senior beagle, was very small and quite shy, not engaging Flossie other than some sniffing.

As I was petting Flossie, they saw the number in her ear. I explained that she had been a laboratory beagle. We had learned from fostering Bailey that companies who use dogs for experiments use numbers to identify the dogs, just like puppy mills. They would also prefer to euthanize them rather than give them to rescue groups. They were afraid the word would get out that they were using dogs in their laboratory, so the rescue groups were sworn to secrecy.

They were smitten—understandably so, and her background and cherry eye did not seem to change that. She was hard to resist. Then within a half-hour of their visit, something happened that shocked all of us. Flossie collapsed on her bed in the driveway and just fell asleep as puppies sometimes do. I know from my only puppy, Snuffy, that puppies play so long and hard and then just crash. While she was dozing, the decision was made to adopt her.

Again, this couple was not ready to take either Starr or Flossie. They wanted them to meet and then would go home and buy leads and beds and get the house ready. Starr would be returned to her foster home, and Flossie would stay with us, at least for the rest of that week. The Mr. said he would pick up Flossie the following Friday.

During that week I wrote them a love letter about Flossie and her quirks. I did so for all the adopters of our fosters, plus I added to this one the need to be patient. I also encouraged them to keep the name Flossie—it fit her so well, but in the end, it was their decision.

The following Friday evening, he arrived and my beloved Flossie left us. Flossie's departure was not like losing Samson or Delilah, but it was still devastating. Tears still come to my eyes when I think of her.

The little nappy that eventually became too small for her little bottom was still on the dryer in the laundry, and every time I saw it, I smiled, remembering her. Yet, I never removed it. I knew deep down it was the best decision for LittleBit and Sophie. I have never been sure it was the best for me.

The next weekend our dear Cayenne also went to her forever home. We would miss them both but happy they would both be in caring homes. Again, we were a family of four. When that would change, we never knew. Once again, we were enjoying our two lovelies.

Well, just the four of us didn't last long. We were asked to foster a female who had been found on the streets. No tags. I'm excited about another floppy-eared dog in our home. In fact, a few days before we were to pick her up, I woke up one morning thinking of her and decided her name should be Emma. EMMA! Where did that come from?

One answer was that I was teaching classes based on the work of Carl Jung, whose wife's name was Emma. I had recently done a play based on the relationship of Emma Jung and Toni Wolf. And then there was my mother's favorite sister and my favorite aunt, Emma. Whatever the reason, Emma was going to be her name.

Oh my, when I saw her, I saw Flossie, although she was not a pup. Long ears, big bulging eyes like Delilah that just pulled me in. Calm and sweet like Sophie.

Emma was bright and easy to train—a pleasure to have in our home. She got along wonderfully with Sophie and LittleBit—a happy pack of girls.

Concerned that she had kennel cough, we took her to our vet. He told us she had a collapsed trachea. She would cough all her life to varying degrees and warned us that in time she might have to take a medication.

Her teeth had a lot of tartar, and he showed us her eyes. "See, her eyes are starting to get a film over them. She's between six or seven."

A few days later, seeing how smitten I was about Emma, David smiled at me and then looked at Emma, "Do you want to adopt her?" I nodded.

Giving up Flossie had been a heartbreak decision, and I could not give up another dog just now. Too many losses in the last few years. We also had said we would not adopt a puppy or any female between one and three years old. That was the gender and age of choice by many adopters, but the older dogs were harder to get adopted. Now, that we knew Emma was between six or seven and she got along so well with our two girls, she was a wonderful addition to our pack.

Again, like LittleBit, we gave Emma to each other for Christmas. We were five once again. Such joy!

As I have mentioned, we rarely heard about our foster dogs after they have left us, but that Christmas I received a three-page letter from Millie's Mom. She included pictures and told me all about Millie's antics, what she loved to do, her daily routine, and how far she had progressed. I was thrilled that she had such caring guardians who loved her to bits.

When I stop to think about the plight of dogs, I become frustrated, confused, bewildered that we call ourselves human, which implies humanity. Yet many animals are treated by humans with such inhumanity. I do not try to put those thoughts aside, knowing there is so much more to be done to help our best friends. That is why I wrote this story of Samson and Delilah and their foster friends.

I wanted to continue to share the story of my two loves. More importantly, I wanted to express and demonstrate to others the joy of having a love affair with dogs and to inspire them to become involved in helping treat dogs more humanely. I encourage you to foster and to rescue. I know you may want that cute little puppy. Resist please and rescue. The money you would have spent donate to a dog rescue.

Dogs enrich our lives and show us kindness and love and understanding, no matter what shape, size, or age, and that does not end with their passing.

All of our dogs and fosters were special, each with endearing quirks. They all left paw prints on my heart. I am grateful that the first twenty fosters I have written about came into our lives.

Above all, I am most grateful to Samson and Delilah. They were incredible ambassadors and had an unselfish spirit that allowed strange dogs to enter our doors again and again. I miss them so, but I know all my dogs will always be with me and are by my side as I write this book.

Please foster. Please rescue.

About Elizabeth Rodenz

Elizabeth has served as a volunteer with several dog rescue organizations, which included fostering and serving as an adoption counselor.

She is the author of *Josephine — A Woman of Indomitable Spirit*, a literary novel. *Samson and Delilah Plus Twenty* is the sequel to her memoir, *Samson and Delilah — My Two Loves*. She is also the author of a fictional tale that teaches personality types based on the work of Swiss psychologist, Carl Jung, *Odd Ducks and Birds of a Feather: A Mystery of Type*.

Elizabeth and David always have a pack of beagles bringing them joy every day.

www.ingramcontent.com/pod-product-compliance
Lightning Source LLC
Chambersburg PA
CBHW071926290426
44110CB00013B/1488